£ 3.95

CONSUMER
BEHAVIOR

EUGENE J. KELLEY, editor
The Pennsylvania State University

PRENTICE-HALL FOUNDATIONS OF MARKETING SERIES

PRENTICE-HALL FOUNDATIONS OF MARKETING SERIES

PRENTICE-HALL, INC., Englewood Cliffs, New Jersey

CONSUMER BEHAVIOR

PETER D. BENNETT

The Pennsylvania State University

HAROLD H. KASSARJIAN

University of California, Los Angeles

Library of Congress Cataloging in Publication Data

BENNETT, PETER D.
 Consumer behavior.

 (Prentice-Hall foundations of marketing series)
 Includes bibliographical references.
 1. Consumers. 2. Consumption (Economics)
Kassarjian, Harold H., joint author. II. Title.
HC79.C6K36   339.4'7   72-731
ISBN 0-13-169383-2

CONSUMER BEHAVIOR

PETER D. BENNETT
The Pennsylvania State University

HAROLD H. KASSARJIAN
University of California

PRENTICE-HALL, INC. Englewood Cliffs, New Jersey

FOUNDATIONS OF MARKETING SERIES

Printed in the United States of America

10 9 8 7 6

PRENTICE-HALL INTERNATIONAL, INC., *London*
PRENTICE-HALL OF AUSTRALIA, PTY., LTD., *Sydney*
PRENTICE-HALL OF CANADA, LTD., *Toronto*
PRENTICE-HALL OF INDIA PRIVATE LIMITED, *New Delhi*
PRENTICE-HALL OF JAPAN, INC., *Tokyo*

FOUNDATIONS OF MARKETING SERIES

The Foundations of Marketing is a series of authoritative and concise books prepared to serve the need for teaching materials incorporating the results of recent research and developments in the study and practice of marketing. The structure of the series—its flexibility within unity of purposes—enables the teacher to construct a complete basic marketing course, adjustable to a level of rigor of the teacher's choosing. Certain or all books can be combined to accomplish individual course objectives. Individual books are self-contained, reasonably complete treatments of the fundamental changes taking place in their areas. Students have the benefits of being introduced to the managerial approach to the field and to the socioeconomic process of marketing by authorities actively engaged in study and research in each field.

An overview of the series and of the managerial approach to marketing is provided by

Marketing Planning and Competitive Strategy

Four books treat important aspects of scientific methodology and decision making in marketing:

Consumer Behavior
Marketing Management and the Behavioral Environment
Men, Motives, and Markets
Quantitative Methods in Marketing

Key policy areas of marketing are covered in

Pricing Decisions and Marketing Policy
Product Policy
Promotion: A Behavioral View

Sales Management
Channel Management
Marketing Logistics
Organizational Buying Behavior

Important environmental areas in marketing are emphasized in

International Marketing, 2nd ed.
Marketing and Public Policy
Marketing in the Canadian Environment

All books may profitably use as supplements

Cases in Marketing Management
Advanced Cases in Marketing Management
History of Marketing

It is hoped that the series will stimulate independent and intelligent thought about the central issues of marketing analysis and policy and that readers will find the books useful guides to a creative and disciplined approach to meeting complex and changing marketing problems.

EUGENE J. KELLEY, *Editor*

The authors wish to acknowledge the careful reviewing of Ben Enis at the University of Houston and the detailed comments on several chapters from Thomas S. Robertson at the University of Pennsylvania. Eugene J. Kelley's help and encouragement is also acknowledged. The clerical assistance of Mrs. Sophia Behrstock and Mrs. Joan Kerstetter was invaluable.

CONTENTS

1

THE STUDY
OF
CONSUMER BEHAVIOR

For as long as there has been exchange of goods and services between buyers and sellers, the ultimate success of all economic activity has depended upon producing goods and services that the buyer considers suitable. Since long before recorded history, buyers have had some freedom of choice in accepting or rejecting the produce of sellers. Even in the most primitive society, attempts to produce and sell products for which buyers have no possible use will meet with utter failure. One can imagine, for example, the absurdity of trying to sell overcoats or automobiles to the Indians in the Amazon jungle where there is neither cold nor roads. This is simply to say that marketers have always been subject to the choice of consumers. Consumer choice has traditionally involved two major decisions—whether or not to buy a particular good or service, and from which of several sellers to buy.

There is nothing new, therefore, about the interest among marketers in the choice behavior of consumers. Why, then, has there been such renewed interest in recent years in the overt concern with consumer behavior among both marketing scholars and practitioners? The answer to that question lies in the realities of the marketplace. The crux of the issue lies in the fact that *freedom* of consumer choice is relative rather than absolute. And the single most important determinant of the freedom of choice is the affluence of consumers and the society in question. One can look across the time dimension in our society and find stages in its development when consumer choice was minimal, when consumers were anxious to consume all that an infant industrial system could produce. When the production capability of an economy is very poorly developed, it may not be able to meet the barest needs of its consumers. In this stage of development, consumers must simply take whatever they can get. This situation generally leads to little real concern with consumers' needs or wishes on the part of producers and marketers, leading Henry Ford to declare that "consumers may have any color automobile they want so long as they want black."

Similarly, one can remain in the present time period and look across the spectrum of highly-developed and underdeveloped nations and see the same conditions. There is only one paper-producing firm in Chile, and there is minimal consumer choice with regard to such products as facial tissue. If the Chilean consumer wishes to use facial tissue, she must choose "Confort," the one and only brand. There is only one producer and marketer of petroleum products in Mexico, the government-owned firm "Pemex." If the Mexicans wish to drive their automobiles, they have no choice but to buy gasoline at their nearest Pemex station. Given these situations, it is easy to understand why the producers of Confort and Pemex may not be deeply concerned with the special wishes or desires of the Chilean or Mexican consumer. They know that these consumers must take whatever they decide to produce.

In the United States, especially during the second half of the twentieth century, neither of the above conditions are prevalent. The productive capacity of this nation at this time far exceeds the minimal level necessary to satisfy the basic needs of the American consumer. At the same time, the bulk of American consumers today have more than adequate income to buy the products and services needed to satisfy their basic needs. There are a host of brands of facial tissue and of gasoline available for the consumer to choose from, so consumer freedom of choice is relatively great. American producers of facial tissue and gasoline (as well as most other products and services) are much more concerned with the specific wishes of consumers than are their counterparts in Chile and Mexico—or than were they themselves in an earlier period of their own history. Confort is cheap, harsh, and comes in one color—white. American consumers, for good or for bad, choose from among a variety of qualities, colors, packages, and even designs when buying facial tissues. Pemex conducts very little research designed to improve the quality of its two gasoline blends. The American consumer today chooses among a variety of blends with an ever-changing array of additives supposedly designed to improve the performance of automobiles.

THE MARKETING CONCEPT: A BLESSING AND A BANE

There has been considerable discussion in marketing literature in recent years about the "marketing revolution." This discussion centers around the need for modern marketing to be consumer-oriented, to be concerned with the needs and wishes of the consumer. All this discussion is rooted in the rapidly expanding freedom of consumer choice among alternative goods and services and among alternative producers of any chosen good or service. Just as Copernicus made us realize that the earth is not the center of the universe but revolves about the sun, we have come to believe that the business firm is not the center of the economic universe but revolves about the consumer. It was estimated several years ago that consumers have the freedom *not* to buy more than forty percent of this nation's total productive capacity.[1] Among the remaining sixty percent, the consumer very rarely does not have the freedom to choose from several alternative producers, although the products often appear to be remarkably similar.

Faced with this seemingly permanent "buyer's market," modern business firms have oriented their operations around what has become known as the *marketing concept*. In what is now the classic presentation of this concept, Levitt made the point clear by distinguishing between the marketing (new) and selling (old) orientations.

> The difference between marketing and selling is more than semantic. *Selling focuses on the needs of the seller; marketing, on the needs of the buyer.* Selling is preoccupied with the seller's need to convert his product into cash; marketing, with the idea of satisfying the needs of the customer by means of the product and the whole cluster of things associated with creating, delivering, and finally consuming it.[2]

The "blessing" in this new orientation is obvious; we see it all around us. As consumers, we enjoy the "color-coordinated pop-up facial tissue box" and the "super-powered gasoline with ML-40." We also enjoy the convenience of the "pop-open aluminum beer can" which we don't have to lug back to the store. But in the last few years, we have had our eyes opened to the "bane" of the marketing concept. Consumers and citizens are the same people; as *citizens*, we don't want to breathe in air that makes living in Los Angeles equivalent to smoking a pack of cigarettes a day. As *consumers*, we don't particularly care if our cars have exhaust emission devices or whether our gasoline is lead-free. As *citizens*, we might. As *consumers*, we like the convenience of aluminum beer cans. As *citizens*, we search for solutions to the growing crisis of solid waste disposal. In the November, 1970, election the people of Washington state voted on a proposition that would require *any* beer or soft drink container to carry a five-cent deposit charge. Here was a chance for people to choose between their convenience as a consumer and their concern for the environment as a citizen. Results: consumers, 52 percent; citizens, 48 percent. This example of people groping for a solution to the dilemma is typical of the ambivalence we face as we work toward a compromise; a similar dilemma confronts marketing strategists.

THE MARKETING CONCEPT AND MARKETING STRATEGY

Marketing strategists are groping for solutions to the conflict between the dictates of the marketing concept, i.e., "satisfying consumers' needs," and the other social responsibilities of the firm. In the process, marketing

---

[1] *Advertising Age* (October 24, 1955).
[2] Theodore Levitt, "Marketing Myopia," *Harvard Business Review* (July-August, 1960), p. 50.

planning requires that peoples' needs as citizens as well as their needs as consumers be considered. Within the constraints of these added responsibilities, however, the basic orientation toward consumer satisfaction will remain, and the need to understand consumer behavior will expand rather than diminish. The practical effects of this new orientation include certain structural changes of business firms, such as bringing previously unrelated functions or departments together under a senior corporate officer at the vice-presidential level. We will not be concerned with those effects in this book, but we will be concerned with the influence this new consumer orientation has had on marketing strategy and planning.

As soon as one becomes serious about consumer orientation, he learns that he does not have *a* market, but that there are a number of *market segments*, each with its own set of needs. As a result, he learns that he does not have *a* marketing plan, but separate marketing plans for the various segments. That is something which, for example, the Scott Paper Company has learned that the Chilean producer of Confort has not yet had reason to learn.

THE INTERDISCIPLINARY APPROACH

A decade ago many of us would have argued that economics was marketing's "mother" discipline. Now we would consider our discipline the melding of all those bodies of knowledge concerned with human behavior—the behavioral sciences. The light that has been shed on human behavior in general by the behavioral sciences is applicable to the study of that subset of behavior exhibited by individuals in their roles as consumers.

The behavioral sciences that have made significant contributions to the study of consumer behavior are economics, sociology, psychology, and to some degree political science and cultural anthropology. The first of these has been most directly concerned with consumer behavior *per se,* while the latter four require considerable interpretation by the student of consumer behavior. Sociology might be said to be concerned with the behavior of groups of individuals, psychology with the individuals themselves, and social psychology and political science with the behavior of individuals within groups or within the group setting. The nature of the present work is necessarily eclectic; it borrows concepts from any and all of these social sciences as it finds them useful.

Much of the content of theory in sociology and psychology deals with abnormal rather than normal behavior. The interest of sociologists with deviant social groups, such as juvenile delinquents, does not provide a great deal of insight into the normal behavior of consumers. The same could be said of the study of abnormal psychology, psychiatry, and psychotherapy. This is *not* to say that we cannot learn something about normal behavior from the study of the abnormal behavior of human beings, or even from the behavior of rats or monkeys, but it does mean that the translation of such findings to the normal is necessary. A great deal of our understanding of psychology, or the behavior of individuals, is based on research conducted with animals and individuals with abnormal behavioral patterns. The applicability of such findings has been interpreted for us and has been quite useful.

A final word about the nature of the behavioral sciences is needed to clarify the nature and the state of development of these sciences from which we will do such heavy borrowing. When compared with certain of the physical sciences, the behavioral sciences may be said to be in their primitive stages of development. One measure of the maturity of a science is its ability to predict the behavior of its subject matter. A chemist can combine certain chemicals or elements and predict with something approaching certainty the behavior of the compound. Our understanding of the laws of physics enables us to predict the trajectory and path of satellites with a great deal of precision. Most prediction in the social sciences, on the other hand, is in probabilistic terms—and with comfortable margins of error.

CONSUMER DECISION PROCESS

A great deal of the research activity in marketing is designed to shed light on the consumer decision process. A few rather elaborate models or theories have been proposed in recent years and numerous lesser or "middle range" theories can be found in the literature. Buying behavior, emerging out of the utility theory of economics, turned first to the traditional stimulus-response views of American psychology. Behavior could be explained simply by stimulus and response, reward and punishment, cues and drives. Complex constructs such as motivation, values, and attitudes, however, could not long be ignored or left implicit. Hence in the 1940's it was the psychoanalytically-oriented motivation researchers who were to introduce and emphasize both conscious and unconscious motivation in marketing.[3] According to these Freudian and neo-Freudian marketing theorists, deep-seated forces led not only to the selection of a spouse but also to the selection of a car, not only to suicide but also to the choice of Sunkist oranges over Florida oranges, not only to thumb sucking but also to the preference of Camel cigarettes over a filtered brand. By the late 1950's mathematical models emerged from what was to become the field of consumer behavior. Again from psychology, the stochastic learning models were adapted to consumer behavior,[4] soon to be followed by cognitive models,[5] flow chart models,[6] and computer simulation ap-

[3] Ernest Dichter, *The Strategy of Desire* (New York: Doubleday & Company, Inc., 1960).

[4] William F. Massy, David B. Montgomery, and Donald G. Morrison, *Stochastic Models of Buying Behavior* (Cambridge, Mass.: The M.I.T. Press, 1970).

[5] Alan R. Andreasen, "Attitudes and Consumer Behavior: A Decision Model," in *New Research in Marketing*, ed. Lee E. Preston (Berkeley: University of California Institute of Business and Economic Research, 1965), pp. 1-16.

[6] James F. Engel, David T. Kollat, and Roger D. Blackwell, *Consumer Behavior* (New York: Holt, Rinehart & Winston, Inc., 1968).

proaches.[7] The discerning student will see traces of each of these approaches woven throughout this book.

From this array of theoretical and empirical contributions we have chosen one model to elaborate in this chapter, that of Howard and Sheth.[8] A brief review of that model will serve two very useful purposes. First, it will begin to indicate just how complex the whole question of consumer behavior really is; and second, it provides something of a framework which ties together the numerous concepts introduced in this volume into a logically consistent whole. The theory is quite complex and not the most appropriate place to be introduced in the study of consumer behavior; for this reason our discussion of it here is necessarily incomplete.

The model is best summarized in Figure 1-1, which is adopted from Howard and Sheth. Note that the diagram includes inputs to and outputs from a complex set of variables (in the rectangular box). The *inputs* are information which can influence the decision process, and the *outputs* are represented by the actual purchase. The rest is the complex process we are interested in understanding.

Inputs. In the Howard-Sheth theory the most significant stimulus display affecting the buyer's behavior consists of information cues about a set of characteristics of the product or brand (quality, price, distinctiveness, service, and availability). These may come to him *from the product itself,* as would occur in the shopping activity, in which case the information cues are *significative.* A similar set of cues could come in *symbolic form* from other impersonal sources such as advertising. Both of these sources are *commercial,* representing the marketing efforts of the firm. The third source is *social* information cues which could affect behavior toward the product or brand and which may come from family, friends, or other members of the groups with which the buyer comes into contact or to which he aspires. This third source differs from the first two in two respects. First, it is *not* commercial; it represents not the firm's marketing activities, but rather conditions over which the marketer has little or no control. And second, the social source is personal while the first two were impersonal.

To elaborate on this model, we can say that these characterize two of the four classes of information sources, which are represented by the shaded areas of Figure 1-2. The sources which have been added help round out the parts of the marketing effort of the firm which may include sales and service personnel with whom the consumer often does have contact. It also points out that there are impersonal, mass media information sources over which the firm has no control.

The purpose for the elaboration of the *inputs* is to tie the study of

[7] Francesco Nicosia, *Consumer Decision Processes* (Englewood Cliffs, N. J.: Prentice-Hall, Inc., 1966); and George H. Haines, Jr., *Consumer Behavior: Learning Models of Behavior* (New York: The Free Press, 1969).

[8] John A. Howard and Jagdish N. Sheth, *The Theory of Buyer Behavior* (New York: John Wiley & Sons, Inc., 1969).

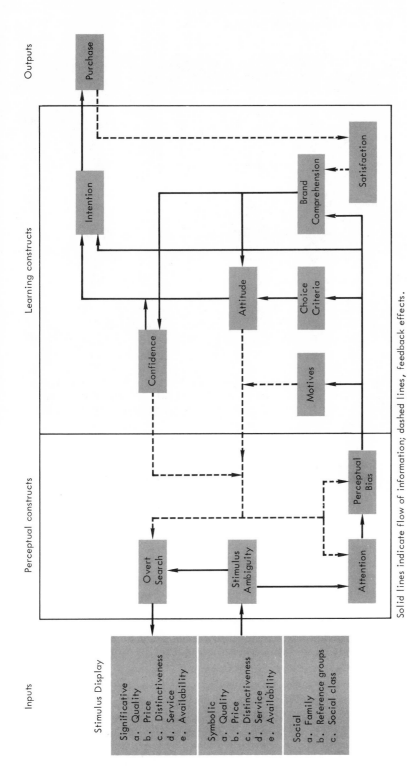

Solid lines indicate flow of information; dashed lines, feedback effects.

FIG. 1-1 A Simplified Description of the Theory of Buyer Behavior

7

	Personal (Social)	Impersonal
Commercial	a. Salesmen b. Service personnel	a. Product (significative) b. Advertising (symbolic)
Noncommercial	a. Family b. Reference groups c. Social class	a. News stories b. Independent testing such as *Consumer Reports*

FIG. 1-2   Information Sources

consumer behavior to the efforts of the marketing manager. The marketing student will recognize here the elements of the *marketing mix*.[9] The information cues include the *price* of the product or brand; they include the quality, distinctiveness, and service aspects of the *product,* which is a source of information cues itself (along with its package); and they include the availability of the product or brand, a result of the firm's *distribution* efforts. Finally, the major commercial information sources are the firm's *promotional* efforts, such as advertising and the activities of the sales forces of the manufacturer and the retailer.

Perceptual Constructs. The first of the two sets of hypothetical constructs in the Howard-Sheth model are those concerned with perception. These concepts pertain to the way the individual deals with information cues from the various sources. One learns that all information available is not attended to *(attention)* and is not always crystal clear in its meaning *(stimulus ambiguity).* Some information cues may bombard the individual without his explicit consent, although he may at times engage in an *overt search* for information. Finally, any information cues to which the individual may attend may be distorted *(perceptual bias)* as a result of his own frame of reference. All of these are complex states or psychological processes and are treated in Chapter 4.[10]

Learning Constructs. The second set of hypothetical constructs in the theory are both more complex and more numerous. Note from Figure 1-1 that the actual *purchase,* the observable behavior, is related to the individual's *intention,* which Howard and Sheth term the "buyer's fore-

[9] For an elaboration of those elements in this series, see Eugene J. Kelley, *Marketing Planning and Competitive Strategy* (Englewood Cliffs, N. J.: Prentice-Hall, Inc., 1972), Chs. 6 and 7.

[10] The determination of the numerous interactions among these complex variables is a major part of *The Theory of Buyer Behavior.* This brief treatment does not pretend to evaluate or critique the theory's validity in whole or part.

cast as to when, where, and how he is likely to buy a brand." The variable *motives* are critical as representations of the goals the individual attempts to achieve through his buying behavior. These goals are derived from his needs, which range from the basic physiological needs (hunger, thirst, sex) to the higher-level learned needs (such as the need for prestige or aesthetic satisfaction). Chapter 5 deals with the concepts of motivation and personality, in some depth.

Most closely related to the buyer's intention is his *attitude* toward the product or brand. As is clear from the model (Figure 1-1), attitudes affect and are affected by a number of the other variables, as well as being quite complex on their own. In fact, another model of the consumer decision process [11] uses the state of the individual's attitudes as the central notion in the model. It should not be surprising, then, that we have devoted Chapter 6 to treatment of attitude structure, attitude formation, and attitude change.

Other learning constructs are *brand comprehension*, "knowledge about the existence and characteristics of those brands that form the buyer's evoked set of alternatives"; *choice criteria*, "the buyer's mental rules, which he utilizes to evaluate brands as goal-objects"; and *confidence*, or "the degree of certainty" the buyer has about his brand comprehension, attitudes, or intentions. Finally, the model includes a construct, *satisfaction*, to refer to the post-purchase and post-use evaluation of the output of the process. This is, of course, the major "feedback" mechanism and is of central importance to *learning* (Chapter 3).

Exogenous Variables. The theory includes a number of variables which are not explained but which do influence some or all of the constructs discussed above and indirectly through those constructs the *output* (purchase). These are taken as "given" and often assumed to be constant. Howard and Sheth include several such concepts which they call *exogenous variables*,[12] some of which are important to us because they have a rich background of theory and research and have been found meaningful in explaining consumer behavior, especially differences among market segments.[13]

1. *Social and organizational setting* is felt to have an important influence on much of the buyer's behavior. The influence of our reference groups on all our behavior speaks cogently of the fact that we are social animals and look at each other for guides regarding what to buy, how to dress, and even how to vote. Chapter 7 is devoted to a closer look at these group influences.

[11] Andreasen, *New Research in Marketing*, pp. 1–16.

[12] Howard and Sheth use the term thus, and warn against confusing it with meaning "outside the body," as it is often used by psychologists or biologists. Howard and Sheth, *The Theory of Buyer Behavior*, p. 58.

[13] We deal here with all but three of these exogenous variables, ignoring *time, pressure,* and *importance of purchase* because they are not dealt with specifically in this volume. We have not included *personality traits* because (1) we consider them inseparable from a discussion of needs and motives, and (2) we would not include them as exogenous.

2. *Social class* is based on a rich research tradition in social stratification. Sociologists have developed copious volumes of information on the influence of social class on all sorts of behavior, and researchers in marketing have found it useful in explaining the behavior of consumers.

3. *Culture*, as we shall define it, is the *shared*, somewhat consistent, patterns of behavior of a group of people. If we say that a person is aggressive, we are referring to a pattern of behavior of an individual— a personality trait. If we say that Americans are materialistic, we are referring to a widely shared pattern of behavior—a culture trait. If we say that first and second generation Americans of Hungarian extraction usually have strong family ties, we are referring to a pattern of behavior broadly shared in a specific subset of the larger culture—a subculture trait. These notions, along with those of social class, are the basis for Chapter 8.

4. *Financial status* refers to "the funds available for purchasing goods and services during some specified time period." [14] Economists have too often overemphasized this variable (along with price, an input variable) to the exclusion of many others. Our response to this overemphasis should *not* be overreaction, as we make more cogent in the following chapter, *Economics of Consumption*, which treats income, wealth, and so on, in the terms of the economic models.

This book is not an advanced treatise dealing with the many fine points of controversy at the cutting edge of basic research in consumer behavior. Rather, it is designed to introduce the students of marketing, economics, and other areas to the modern approach to the study of consumer behavior. We seek to present concisely the most substantial of the many concepts from several disciplines which have been found meaningful.

---

[14] Howard and Sheth, *The Theory of Buyer Behavior*, p. 78.

2

THE ECONOMICS
OF
CONSUMPTION

We mentioned in the preceding chapter that there has been a recent blossoming of interest in consumer behavior in the academic community. We also indicated that the modern approach to studying this complex subject is "interdisciplinary," involving concepts from all the social sciences concerned with human behavior. This chapter will lay out the elements of a "unidisciplinary" theory of consumer behavior.[1] Why?

We do it for two reasons, each of which is important enough to justify its early presentation. First, the economic theory of consumer behavior is one of the most completely refined bodies of theory in the social sciences. It has a long history, first introduced in the original economic treatise by Adam Smith, *Wealth of Nations*, in 1776. It has occupied a central role in microeconomic theory and has attracted the attention of some of the finest minds in the discipline. While we will find it necessary later to discard it as a complete explanation of consumer behavior, it does make important contributions. We therefore do not wish to be guilty of "throwing out the baby with the bathwater." Second, we feel that the student will more thoroughly understand the contributions from the other behavioral sciences once he is acquainted with the "traditional" theory, sees its untenable assumption which is derived from thinking of consumer behavior as only an economic phenomenon, and understands that the recent modern treatment of the subject is largely a revolt from this traditional theory.

[1] For a more complete, but still elementary presentation, see David Hamilton, *The Consumer in Our Economy* (Boston: Houghton Mifflin Company, 1962); or Willard W. Cochrane and Carolyn Shaw Bell, *The Economics of Consumption* (New York: McGraw-Hill Book Company, Inc., 1956). A more sophisticated treatment is available in Richard H. Leftwich, *The Price System and Resource Allocation* (New York: Holt, Rinehart & Winston, Inc., 1966), Chs. 4 and 5.

THE UNIVERSALITY OF THE CHOICE PROBLEM

One of the basic assumptions underlying the theory is that consumer behavior always involves choice. This is derived from the belief that (1) each consuming unit has a limited (finite) income, (2) each consuming unit has unlimited (infinite) needs or wants, and (3) each good or service capable of satisfying a need or want carries a nonzero cost. In short, few of us are capable of consuming all the goods and services we would like to have and must, therefore, choose among them. We further assume that each consuming unit will tend to maximize its total satisfaction by spreading its choices among those goods and services that yield, *for it,* the greatest amount of satisfaction.

Jeremy Bentham, the noted nineteenth-century utilitarian, assumed that man was essentially hedonistic and would always act to maximize his pleasure and to minimize his pain, and pleasure yields *utility* and pain yields *disutility!* The crux of the theory of consumer behavior, then, is that the consumer attempts to maximize his utility. Now we have used both the words "satisfaction" and "utility" to define that which consumers wish to maximize. The two are related in such a way that we can speak of utility as a measure of the satisfaction of needs and wants. The imaginary unit of measure we shall use is called a *util;* we may speak of a certain mix of goods and services consumed as providing, for example, 5, 10, or 100 *utiles.*

THE LAW OF DIMINISHING MARGINAL UTILITY

The basic principle that explains the way consumers choose a certain mix of goods and services is called the *law of diminishing marginal utility,* which is derived from the belief that an individual's ability to enjoy the use of a good diminishes as he consumes more of that good. Using men's belts as an example, this means that the first belt that a man owns provides him with a great deal of utility. Not only might it be an attractive addition to his costume, but it is needed to keep his trousers up. A second belt might be very useful also, if the individual desires to match different color suits, shoes, and so forth. The first belt, a black one, provides both the utility gained from keeping one's trousers up and utility of properly matched attire. Although the second belt, a brown one, is not needed to keep the trousers up, it still provides a great deal of utility in its function of matching an outfit. A third belt would be nice to have and may provide still more variety and thus some utility. The same may be true for fourth and fifth belts of different styles and colors. One eventually reaches a point, however, where the addition of another belt to the wardrobe becomes more of a nuisance than a satisfaction: it just takes up more closet space.

What we have said by this example is that as the number or quantity of a good consumed increases, the total utility gained by the increase in that quantity increases at a decreasing rate. Now if we define *marginal utility* as that extra bit of utility provided by consuming one more unit of a good, we see that as the quantity consumed increases, the marginal utility declines. Table 2-1 and Figures 2-1 and 2-2 demonstrate the law of diminishing marginal utility more clearly.

TABLE 2-1

Quantity of a Good (Belts) Consumed	Total Utility (Utiles)	Marginal Utility (Utiles)
0	0	
1	10	10
2	18	8
3	24	6
4	28	4
5	30	2
6	30	0

Figure 2-1 depicts the principle that, as more of a good is consumed, total utility increases at a decreasing rate. Whether or not any particular individual reaches a saturation point at six or some other number of belts is not at issue. The *shape* of the curve indicates that all of us will at some point reach the condition where the addition of another belt (or any other good) will add nothing to our total utility. Figure 2-2 is derived directly from Figure 2-1. The downward-sloping marginal utility curve shows that the utility added by *one more* of a good decreases as the quantity of the good consumed increases.

The law of diminishing marginal utility does not hold just for belts, of course. Most of us would like to consume at least one steak dinner each week. A second steak each week adds to total utility, but not so much as the first. The marginal utility of steak decreases and will reach a point where we are so sick of steak that consuming one more will *add* nothing to our total utility and may even *subtract* from it. The same principle holds true for goods and services ranging from Cokes to fur coats or automobiles.

THE LAW OF EQUAL MARGINAL UTILITY PER DOLLAR

Now if we take the law of diminishing marginal utility as given, and if we accept the fact that an individual will attempt to maximize his total utility, given limited income, we can explain the individual's division of expenditure. The consuming unit will allocate its finite income in such a way that the utility received from the last unit of expenditure

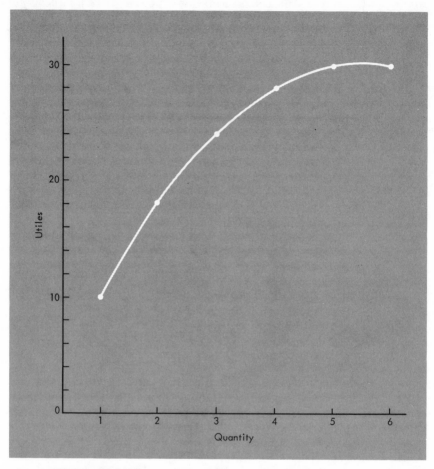

FIG. 2-1 Total Utility

(the last dollar spent) is equal for each good. Stated another way, the individual will allocate his income so that the marginal utility per dollar is equal for all goods and services—the *law of equal marginal utility per dollar.*

It is obvious that since the prices of goods and services differ, a direct comparison of the utility of different goods is impossible. One dollar spent on chewing gum probably far exceeds the typical consumer's desire for gum, while one dollar spent for an automobile will not begin to make a down payment. We must therefore find some scheme for making various goods at various prices comparable. We do this with a measure called *weighted marginal utility,* or the number of utiles provided by the last unit consumed divided by the price of the unit. To return to our belt example, the actual marginal utility (number of utiles added to the total) of the third belt was six; if the belts cost $3.00 each, the weighted

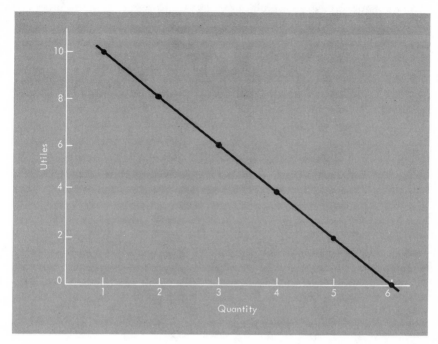

FIG. 2-2 Marginal Utility

marginal utility of the third belt is 2.00. Since the marginal utility of the fourth belt was four utiles, the weighted marginal utility of that belt is 1.33. The student should be able to see that the weighted marginal utility function is downward-sloping just as was the marginal utility function. (Mathematically, then, if we divide a function by a constant ($3.00), we do not change the general shape of the curve.)

Now if we divide the marginal utilities of all competing goods and services by their respective prices, we will be able to compare weighted marginal utilities. Let us illustrate the concept by assuming that an individual must allocate his income between two competing goods, product X and product Y. At some point on the utility function, the marginal utility of X is 30 utiles and its price is $3.00; product X, then, has a weighted marginal utility at that point of 10.00. At some point, the marginal utility of product Y is 40 utiles and its price is $5.00, giving it a weighted marginal utility at that point of 8.00. Since the weighted marginal utility of X is greater than Y, it will be to the best interest of the consumer to shift some expenditure from Y to X. The shift in income allocation from Y to X will continue until the weighted marginal utilities of both products are equal. As the consumer shifts expenditures from goods with a relatively low marginal utility to goods with a relatively high marginal utility, he increases his *total* utility, which we have assumed he is trying to do.

As the consumer shifts purchases away from product Y, he reduces the quantity of that product consumed. Based on our accepted principle of declining (downward-sloping) marginal utility, the shift, *away from* product Y causes an *increase* in its marginal utility. Likewise, a shift *toward* product X causes a *decrease* in its marginal utility. At some point, the rising marginal utility of Y will become equal to the falling marginal utility of X. At that point, the allocation of income to the two products is ideal, and total utility will be maximized.

A simple example will serve to illustrate this very important point. Assume again two products, X and Y, with prices of $1.00 and $2.00, respectively. Assume also that the utility functions for these two products are as indicated in Table 2-2. Let us further assume that the con-

TABLE 2-2

Product X, price $1.00				Product Y, price $2.00			
Quantity Consumed	Total Utility	Marginal Utility	Weighted Marginal Utility	Quantity Consumed	Total Utility	Marginal Utility	Weighted Marginal Utility
1	9	9	9.00	1	25	25	12.50
2	17	8	8.00	2	45	20	10.00
3	24	7	7.00	3	60	15	7.50
4	30	6	6.00	4	70	10	5.00
5	35	5	5.00	5	75	5	2.50
6	39	4	4.00	6	75	0	0.00
7	42	3	3.00				
8	44	2	2.00				
9	45	1	1.00				
10	45	0	0.00				

sumer has a total of $13.00 to allocate between these two products, and that the first allocation is to purchase 6 of product Y and 1 of product X ($6 \times \$2.00 + 1 \times \$1.00 = \$13.00$). At this point, the weighted marginal utility of X is 9.00 and that of Y is 0.00. It thus behooves the consumer to shift some of his expenditure from Y (the good with the low-weighted marginal utility) to X. Let a shift in this direction take place so that the consumer buys 5 of Y and 3 of X ($5 \times \$2.00 + 3 \times \$1.00 = \$13.00$). After the shift, the weighted marginal utility of X is 7.00 and that of Y is 2.50. We conclude then that even further shifts from Y to X are in order.

Before the shift, total utility consisted of 9 utiles from product X and 75 utiles from product Y, for a total of 84 utiles. After the shift, total utility consisted of 99 utiles, 24 from X and 75 from Y. Acting in his best interests, this consumer will shift even more of his expenditures from Y to X. Let another shift in this direction take place so that the consumer buys 4 of product Y and 5 of product X ($4 \times \$2.00 + 5 \times \$1.00 = \$13.00$). Now total utility amounts to 105 utiles (35 from X and 70 from Y), and the weighted marginal utilities of X and Y are equal at 5.00. The theory tells us that we have reached the ideal allocation of expenditure between X and Y, that point where total utility is maximized.

Let us test this statement by making one more shift from Y to X. Let the consumer shift so that he buys 3 of Y and 7 of X ($3 \times \$2.00 + 7 \times \$1.00 = \$13.00$). Total utility now is 102 (42 from X and 60 from Y), less than the total utility of 105 obtained from consuming 4 of X and 5 of Y; the weighted marginal utility of X is 3.00 and of Y is 7.50. This indicates that a shift back from X to Y is in order.

This example serves to illustrate the general principle, but does so only for the allocation of fixed income to two products. The more general proposition concerning all products may be written as follows. The individual should allocate his income so that the weighted marginal utility $\left(\dfrac{\text{marginal utility}}{\text{price}}\right)$ for each and every good is equal:

$$\frac{MU_x}{P_x} = \frac{MU_y}{P_y} = \ldots = \frac{MU_n}{P_n}$$

If any good gave more marginal utility per dollar of price than the common marginal utility per dollar, the consumer could increase total utility by allocating more income to it and less to other goods. If any good gave less marginal utility per dollar than the common marginal utility per dollar, he could increase total utility by allocating less to it and more to other goods.

THE INDIFFERENCE APPROACH

One of the problems which long troubled economists was that this theory required the measurement of utility, an intrinsically nonmeasurable concept. In 1939 J. R. Hicks presented the first systematic treatment of the *indifference approach* to the explanation of consumer behavior, an approach which no longer required that assumption. This new approach did not deny the concept of utility, but rather only that it had to be measured on a *cardinal* scale, that is, the number of utiles; it assumes instead that utility can be measured on an *ordinal* scale—that is, one can say simply that he *prefers* something to something else.[2]

Let us return to our imaginary products, X and Y, for an explanation of the indifference approach. This explanation gets its name from the proposition that the consumer recognizes when he prefers some combination of X and Y to another, and when he is *indifferent* to combinations of X and Y. In Figure 2-3 the combinations of the products are represented in the form (1,10), meaning 1 of X and 10 of Y. The solid line in the

[2] J. R. Hicks, *Value and Capital* (New York: Oxford University Press, 1939), Part I.

figure is an *indifference curve*. The consumer is indifferent to any and all combinations which fall on this curve: he would just as soon have 1 X and 10 Y's as 3 X's and 6 Y's or 5 X's and 4 Y's or 9 X's and 3 Y's. Any combination to the "northeast" of that curve, represented by the △ (7,6), 7 of X and 6 of Y, is preferred to combinations on it. Any combination to the "southwest" represented by the small squares, □ (1,6), etc., is less desirable. The broken line in Figure 2-3 represents the *budget constraint*, or the maximum amount the consumer can spend on X and Y. Recall earlier that the price of X is $1.00 and the price of Y is $2.00. If the consumer has $13.00 to spend and buys all X's, he can have 13; if he buys only Y, he can have 6.5. Check back to see that all the points, (1,6), (3,5), and (7,3), are all combinations which have lower total utility than (5,4),[3] but which all fall on the budget constraint of $13.00. The obvious conclusion, then, is that the consumer's utility is maximized where *the budget constraint is tangent to the indifference curve*. To consume any other combination of X and Y on the indifference curve in Figure 2-3 could cost more than $13.00 and yield exactly the same satisfaction.

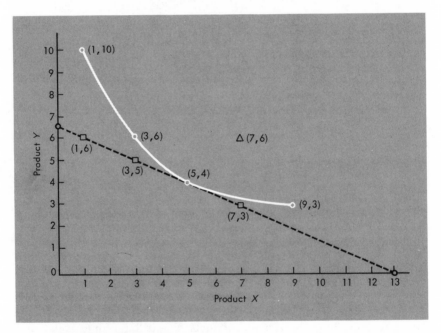

FIG. 2-3   Indifference Curve

The Indifference Map. The fact that we have combinations of X and Y, such as △(7,6), which we prefer to any combination on the indif-

---

[3] This illustrates that the concept of diminishing marginal utility is carried over into the indifference approach. It is interesting to prove from that fact that indifference curves are always convex to the origin of the chart.

ference curve, and that there are less-preferred combinations, such as ☐(3,5), shows that our indifference curve is one member of a family of such curves. We refer to this as the *indifference map,* illustrated in Figure 2-4. All points on curve I_4 have equal preference, and all are preferred to the combinations falling on I_3, which are all preferred to those on I_2, and so on.

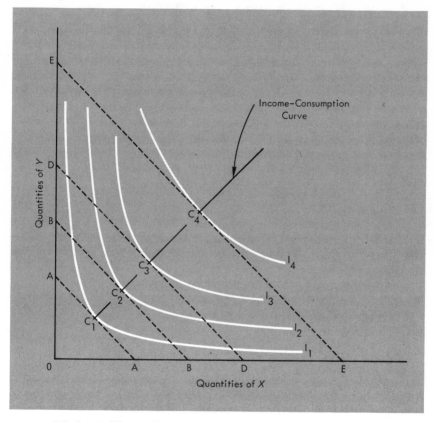

FIG. 2-4 Indifference Map

If the consumer's budget constraint is small, such as is represented by **AA**, he will consume that combination on I_1 where it is tangent to **AA**, point C_1. As the budget constraint rises to **BB** tangent to I_2, **DD** tangent to I_3, and **EE** tangent to I_4, the combinations consumed change to C_2, C_3, and C_4. The line that connects these points is referred to as the *income-consumption* curve, because it relates changes in income (budget constraint) to changes in consumption of products X and Y.

It should be obvious that the *slope* of the budget constraint is a function of the relative prices of X and Y. The slope of the budget constraint in Figure 2-3 represents the fact that the prices of X and Y are $1.00 and $2.00, respectively.

Now examine Figure 2-5, where the indifference map remains unchanged from Figure 2-4, and see what happens when *prices* are changed. Given this indifference map, and assuming a budget constraint of **AA**, the combination of X and Y consumed will be at C_1 on indifference curve

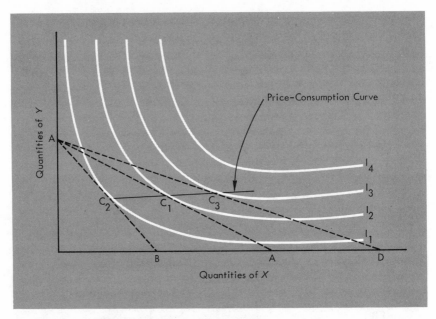

FIG. 2-5   Indifference Map with Price Change

I_2, all from what we have said before. Let us assume the price of X is raised. The budget constraint will shift to **AB**. The price increase in one of the products took us down to a lower indifference curve (I_1), with lower levels of consumption of both X and Y. Now, let us assume that, instead of rising, the price of X decreases. The price decrease shifts the budget constraint from **AA** to **AD**. More of both products is consumed (C_3) on a higher indifference curve, I_3. The line formed by connecting C_1, C_2, and C_3 is the *price-consumption curve* for X, since it *relates changes in quantities consumed with changes in prices of* X.

The changes in the quantities consumed of these two products come from two effects of the price change: the income effect and the substitution effect. When the price of something consumed goes down and there is no change in actual *money* income, *real* income goes up. Additional amounts of X and Y are consumed partially because of this increase in real income ($C_3 - C_1$) (this part of the increase is said to be due to the *income effect*); and partially because since the price of X has been reduced relative to Y (and all other products), one is likely to spend more on it instead of on other things (this portion of the increased consumption of X is said to be due to the *substitution effect*). Now, simply reverse the procedure for the price increase. The increase causes a drop in real income; less of X and Y is consumed, partly due to the income effect and partly due to the substitution effect (both negative this time).

Just as with the marginal utility approach, the indifference analysis can be expanded beyond two products to the consideration of many products. Visualize the three-product case, where indifference curves in two-dimensional space have now been converted into indifference "bowls" in three-dimensional space. When we must deal with n products in n-dimensional space, geometric analogies wear thin—perhaps just when the visualizer's patience wears thin.

CONSUMER AND MARKET DEMAND

Consumer demand is the quantity of a good or service the consumer is willing to buy at varying prices. We shall see that consumer demand can be derived from the foregoing theory of consumer behavior. First, we must think of money as a "good" or representative of "all other goods" in explaining the demand for X. As such, money is subject to the law of diminishing marginal utility, i.e., the more money owned, the less its marginal utility—just as with belts, steaks, and so on.

Now consider Figure 2-6. Note its similarity to Figure 2-5, but now product Y is money itself. Assuming no change in income, the budget

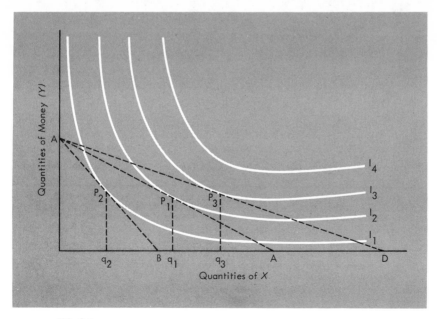

FIG. 2-6

constraint **AA** determines the quantity of X which will be bought (q_1) at the given price (p_1). If the price of X rises to p_2, the quantity bought will drop to q_2. If the product's price is lowered to p_3, consumption rises to q_3. Just as in the case of shifts in the quantities consumed of two products (see Figure 2-5), the changes in quantities of money and one product resulting from price changes are due partly to the *income effect* and partly to the *substitution effect*. As a reminder, the income effect occurs with a drop in price because the consumer's actual money income has remained the same, while the price of the product he buys has been reduced, thus increasing his real income. The substitution effect occurs with the lower price because X provides the consumer more utility per dollar than other products, causing him to shift some expenditures from them to X.

When we convert the points on Figure 2-6, which represent quantities of X purchased $(q_1, q_2, \text{ and } q_3)$, to a scale relating them to levels of price, we have the familiar downward-sloping demand curve in Figure 2-7. The logic of its downward slope derives directly from the income and substitution effects. Now this demand by a single consumer can be

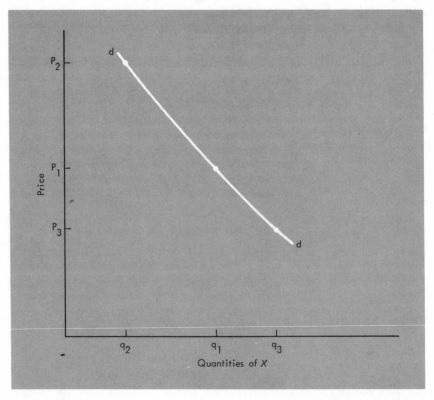

FIG. 2-7

converted into a market demand simply by adding up all the consumer demand functions. *Market demand* is the quantity of a good or service that all consumers in the market stand ready to buy at varying prices.

EVALUATION OF THE ECONOMIC DEMAND

We said earlier that there is value in this traditional theory of consumer behavior; that value lies primarily in its partial explanation of the complex phenomenon with which it deals. There is some truth in the notion that consumers try to maximize their satisfaction. There is some truth in the notions of diminishing marginal utilities and downward-sloping demand curves. Any East Texas farmer can tell you that as the price of something goes up, fewer of it is going to be bought, and vice versa. Unlike what they have often been accused of, economists have never really thought that consumers were "rapid calculators of pleasures and pain," adding up utiles, much less computing marginal utility.

We also said earlier that we would finish by having to reject this theory as an adequate explanation of how consumers behave. We do this for three major reasons.[4]

1. *The theory is not operational.* In a real sense the theory is more a *normative* model than a *positive* model. By that we mean it attempts to explain how a consumer *ought to* behave, rather than how he does behave. As a normative model, however, it simply cannot be applied to real world situations because we are not able to measure utility.

> The theory of consumer behavior as it stands now cannot be used to recommend adjustments in consumption patterns, *because where the results of those adjustments cannot be measured, it is impossible to say whether the recommended pattern of consumption yields more or less satisfaction than the previous pattern to the consumer involved.*[5]

2. *The theory is centered on the product, not the consumer.* The economic theory views utility as a function of the good consumed. A simple psychological notion would help the economist. We can properly classify consumption behavior as *goal-directed* behavior: the consumer buys and consumes products to satisfy certain needs. The psychologist would distinguish between the *goal* of saitsfying those needs, and the *goal-object* (product), which is the mechanism through which the goal is reached. This view would shift some focus away from the product and toward the consumer's needs and motives (see Chapter 5).

This problem with the economic theory is partially softened by the recent work of Lancaster, an economist who described the theory as "an

---

[4] There are more problems with the theory than these three, some technical, such as the problem of indivisibility of products (it is difficult to buy half of an automobile). These others are insignificant, however, compared to the three discussed.

[5] Cochrane and Bell, *The Economics of Consumption,* p. 144 (emphasis in the original).

example of how to extract the minimum of results from the minimum of assumptions." [6] In his own words, the major contribution in his new approach "lies in breaking away from the traditional approach that goods are the direct objects of utility and, instead, supposing that it is the *properties* or *characteristics* of the goods from which utility is derived." [7] This emphasis permits dealing with the need-satisfying attributes of the good, and opens the door to a reconsideration of the theory. Unfortunately, he partially closes the door again by assuming that the attributes which a product possesses are intrinsic and are so recognized by all consumers. This, of course, is untenable in light of what we know about perception and perceptual bias (see Chapter 4).

3. *The theory is simply incomplete.* Consumer behavior is an extremely complex subject, and we have just begun to understand it. A lesson we have learned very well, although most economists apparently refuse to incorporate it, is that no one discipline will be adequate to the task. The economist assumes that consumers have perfect information or that they all have the same information. He thereby ignores all we have learned about selective perception and how individuals use information in dealing with perceived risk (Chapter 4). He assumes that consumers' tastes and preferences are constant, and he thereby ignores the simplest notions of learning (Chapter 3) and of attitude formation and change (Chapter 6).

A noted exception to this group of unidiscipline advocates is Professor Martin Shubik of Yale. He recently said that his objection to the received theory was not that it did not add to economic knowledge, but that "it is presented to students of microeconomics as though it were *the relevant* way to study consumer behavior, rather than one partially explored path in almost virgin territory." [8]

It is surely obvious from even the brief treatment of the economic theory in this chapter that *price* and *income* are the only factors affecting consumer choice which the economist does not simply sweep under the rug. Or, as Shubik expressed it, "Empirically, the question boils down to how much variance can be explained by price and income information."

No theory which deals with only one aspect of the individual consumer (income), while ignoring other often more important aspects, such as personality, attitudes, and social class, can be considered adequate. No theory which deals with only one aspect of the marketing activities (price) that impinge on the consumer, while ignoring others such as product variations and innovation, distribution systems, and marketing communications can be considered adequate. As Shubik says,

> To many economists advertising is a dirty word. We draw a demand curve on the blackboard, look wisely at the class, and say that advertising shifts this demand curve. We go to the board and draw another line showing that the demand has been shifted. How it is shifted, why it is shifted, what are the

---

[6] Kelvin J. Lancaster, "A New Approach to Consumer Theory," *Journal of Political Economy,* Vol. 74 (April, 1966), 132.

[7] Lancaster, *Journal of Political Economy,* Vol. 74, 133 (emphasis added).

[8] Martin Shubik, "A Curmudgeon's Guide to Microeconomics," *The Journal of Economic Literature,* Vol. 8 (June, 1970), 410.

underlying mechanisms—these questions we leave implicitly as exercises for the students. This treatment of advertising reminds me of the story about the owl who was the wisest creature in the forest. A centipede with ninety-nine sore feet came to consult with the owl. The advice he was given was to walk one inch above the ground for the next two weeks in order to give his sore feet enough time to heal. The centipede observed that it was a splended [sic] suggestion, was precise, insightful and logical. He then asked the owl, "How am I going to walk one inch above the ground?" The owl replied, "I have solved your conceptual problem. Do not bother me with technical details." [9]

AGGREGATE DATA ON EXPENDITURES

We should remind the reader again not to let the critical appraisal of the economic theory of consumer behavior blind him to its contribution to the more complete interdisciplinary explanation. Income does make a difference. Return a moment to the income-consumption curve in Figure 2-4. Aggregate data on expenditures of households by varying levels of income is published regularly by the U. S. Bureau of Labor Statistics. Household expenditures in absolute dollars increase as income increases for all classes of goods, supporting the notion of the income-consumption curve. The *proportion* spent on various categories adds additional insights. In the middle of the nineteenth century, a Prussian government statistician named Ernst Engel supplied empirical evidence for an obvious fact: poor people spend a larger share of their total incomes for food than do rich people. More precisely, as income rises, the proportion spent for food declines.

Engel's law grew into Engel's laws as others elaborated on the relationship between income and expenditures for various categories of expenditures. These laws might be summarized as follows:

1. As income rises, the proportion spent on food declines.
2. As income rises, the proportion spent on housing and household goods remains about the same.
3. As income rises, the proportion spent on clothing stays the same or perhaps rises slightly.
4. As income rises, the proportion spent on luxuries rises.

The laws are continually put to the test, and though they are sometimes broken, they generally hold true. A major study of post-World War II data from some thirty-seven countries found some cross-cultural support for them.[10]

While we have not been able to accept the economist's theory of consumer behavior as sufficient, it is a useful point of departure. It forms a backdrop for contributions from the other behavioral sciences dealt with in the following chapters.

[9] Shubik, *The Journal of Economic Literature*, 422.
[10] Hendrik Houthakker, "An International Comparison of Household Expenditure Patterns, Commemorating the Centenary of Engel's Law," *Econometrica* (October, 1957), pp. 532-51.

Summary

1. Consumer behavior always involves *choice;* we are not able to consume all the goods and services we would like and must choose among them.

2. *Total utility* (satisfaction), derived from consuming more and more of a good, increases at a decreasing rate.

3. *Marginal utility* (the satisfaction derived from consuming one more unit of a good) declines as more units are consumed.

4. *Weighted marginal utility* (the marginal utility per dollar spent) will be the same for all products where the consumer's total utility is maximized.

5. The *indifference approach* was developed because it does not assume that utility can be measured; rather, the consumer need only be able to recognize when he is indifferent to various combinations of products. All combinations for which he is indifferent comprise an *indifference curve.*

6. The *budget constraint* is the total money available to the consumer to spend on the different products. Total utility is maximized at that combination of products where the budget constraint is tangent to a utility curve.

7. The *income-consumption curve* is comprised of the combinations the consumer can afford as his budget constraint changes, and as he moves from one indifference curve to another on the *indifference map.* The income-consumption curve relates changes in consumption with changes in income.

8. The *price-consumption curve* is comprised of the combinations the consumer can afford as the price of one product changes, and he moves from one indifference curve to another. The price-consumption curve relates changes in consumption to changes in prices of one product.

9. The changes in the combinations consumed which make up the price-consumption curve are attributable to both the *income effect* (changes in *real* income as prices change and *money* income remains constant), and to the *substitution effect* (changes in the combination of products consumed due to changes in their relative prices).

10. The typical downward-sloping *consumer demand curve* is derived directly from the indifference approach simply by making one of the "products" money itself and finding the price consumption curve for changes in the price of the other product. The *market demand curve* is derived from the sum of all consumer demand curves.

11. The theory does have value as a partial explanation of consumer behavior; it must be rejected as an adequate theory, however, because (1) it is *not operational,* (2) it is centered on the *product* and not the *consumer,* and (3) it is *incomplete,* dealing only with price and income influences, ignoring many other individual and marketing variables.

3

LEARNING
TO
CONSUME

For two reasons we begin our treatment of the constructs upon which the modern understanding of consumer behavior is built with *learning*. First, it will help underscore a major problem with the economic theory: we can never treat tastes and preferences as static. Second, and more importantly, learning is considered by many psychologists to be the most fundamental process in human behavior. Throughout this text the process of learning will continually crop up as we discuss the development of attitudes or the determinants of perception. We shall see that a major (and highest-order) class of motives or needs are *learned* needs. As we study the influences of groups, social class, and culture, we will see that the control they exert over the behavior of the individual is through norms of behavior; this influence occurs because the individual internalizes (*learns*) those norms.

We will first deal with some aspects of *learning theory*, including formal definitions, some conflicts among learning theories, and some fundamentals of the learning process. The second part of the chapter will treat the *marketing implications* of learning theory, their rich potential for explaining the development of brand loyalty, and their influence on consumer information-seeking behavior and in advertising.

Learning Theory

Since learning is central to the study of human behavior, and since it embraces a number of more-or-less conflicting theories, it is not surprising that a precise definition is hard to nail down. For reasons which will be clear soon, we supply two:

> *Definition I:* "Learning refers to a more or less permanent change in behavior which occurs as a result of practice." [1]

[1] Gregory A. Kimble, *Hilgard and Marquis' Conditioning and Learning* (2nd ed.) (New York: Appleton-Century-Crofts, Inc., 1961), p. 2.

Definition II: "Learning is the process by which an activity originates or is changed through reacting to an encountered situation. . . ." [2]

The learning of facts or skills, as the term is often used by nonpsychologists, is included but is just a small portion of what is learned. We must recognize that "change in behavior" means more than just the overt acts of the individual which can be observed. It includes changes in *verbal* behavior which may indicate more fundamental changes in attitudes, motives, or even personality.

WHAT IS LEARNED?

We cannot deal with this question without some elaboration on conflicting learning theories, particularly the conflicts between the *stimulus-response* and the *cognitive* schools. The former (S-R) school claims that what we learn are habits, or links of particular responses with particular stimuli. Through the repetitive linking of a response to a stimulus, the probability of the response's being elicited by the stimulus increases. For example, as the number of times a rat runs a simple T-maze increases, the probability of his taking the appropriate turn increases. Or as the number of times a consumer purchases a particular brand of a product increases, the probability of his purchasing that brand the next time he needs the product increases.

S-R theorists are separated into (at least) two camps. *Reinforcement* theorists insist that learning occurs only in the presence of reinforcement, i.e., reward or punishment. The classic statement on which this school is based is Thorndike's classic *Law of Effect:*

> The law of Effect is that: Of several responses made to the same situation, those which are accompanied or closely followed by satisfaction to the animal will, other things being equal, be more firmly connected with the situation, so that, when it recurs, they will be more likely to recur; those which are accompanied or closely followed by discomfort to the animal will, other things being equal, have their connections with that situation weakened, so that, when it recurs, they will be less likely to occur. The greater the satisfaction or discomfort, the greater the strengthening or weakening of the bond.[3]

Basing our assumptions on this law, we would conclude that the rat would learn when he was rewarded (as with food) for taking the right turn, and punished (as with an electric shock) when he took the wrong turn. Similarly, we would conclude that the consumer's probability of

[2] Ernest R. Hilgard and Gordon H. Bower, *Theories of Learning* (3rd ed.) (New York: Appleton-Century-Crofts, Inc., 1966), p. 2. This definition and the other omit changes that are due to native response tendencies, maturation, or temporary states of the organism, such as fatigue or drug influence.

[3] Edward L. Thorndike, *Animal Intelligence* (New York: The Macmillan Co., 1911), p. 244.

repeating a brand's purchase would increase if he were satisfied with the purchase and decrease if he were dissatisfied.

A second camp of S-R theorists, the *contiguity* theorists, argue that learning takes place without reinforcement; they claim that an association between stimulus and response occurs when the two occur together in time, i.e., are contiguous to each other. They are not able to deny the strengthening effect of reinforcement, however. Guthrie argued that simultaneous S-R occurrences completed the learning effect, while any reward present simply prevented forgetting or kept the association from being unlearned.[4]

The cognitive theorists disagree with both schools of S-R theory. This group says that what we learn are cognitive structures. That rat did not blindly develop a habit of turning toward food. Without its being anthropomorphic, we can claim he learned something like, "If I turn one way, I'm going to find some food and if I turn the other I will get a shock. Food is good and the electric shock hurts, so I'm going to find that turn where the food is." The consumer experienced the brand of the product he purchased. It met his needs quite well, and some other brand may not, so he determines to purchase the same brand rather than running the risk of an unsatisfactory purchase.

It is probably wise for students of consumer behavior to remain eclectic in their approach to learning theory, picking those constructs from each which best fit the problem at hand. While it is an unsettled issue, it is probably true there is more than one answer to the question, "What is learned?" S-R theory may adequately explain the habitual purchase of toothpaste, and cognitive theory may better explain the complexities of buying a home.

HOW DO WE LEARN?

The influence of S-R theories of learning for years answered that question—"through trial and error." Past experience is the key to learning, and Definition I above fits this school of thought quite well. The traditional theories growing out of Thorndike's Law of Effect held the rather mechanistic view based on impressive experimental evidence, mostly with lower-order animals from rats to cats, of learning's being the product of a number of trials.

During the 1920's, *Gestalt* psychology made an important impact on American theorists through the influence of four German psychologists.[5]

> Koffka's book had an important effect upon American learning theory because of its detailed criticism of trial-and-error learning as conceived by Thorndike—a thrust at the very heart of the currently popular theory. . . . Köhler's book brought the notion

---

[4] Edwin R. Guthrie, "Association and the Law of Effect," *Psychological Review*, Vol. 47 (1940), 127-48.

[5] Max Wertheimer, Kurt Koffka, Wolfgang Köhler, and Kurt Lewin. (Gestalt psychologists are a subset of the cognitive school.)

of insightful learning into the foreground, as an alternative to trial and error.[6]

Köhler's experiments with primates had shown the possibility for *insightful* learning, where apes "reasoned" through a problem of getting to food through using a stick as an extension of their arm, through stacking boxes to reach food placed high, and even through attaching two sticks together when either one was too short to reach the food. All this *without* trial and error, and all somewhat obvious. "Insight was not a new discovery—it was a return to a conception laymen had never abandoned."[7]

Gestalt theory was rooted in the notion that our perceptions of things are not in terms of individual characteristics, such as color, smell, and the like, but rather as a whole entity. Stimuli form patterns, and it is upon organization of complex stimulus sets that our experience depends. The word *Gestalt* means *form* or *configuration;* an extension of Gestalt theory is *field theory,* which leads its advocates to hold that learning, too, is rooted in the current phenomenal field and not on a series of past S-R links.

But is there a common meeting ground for these two conflicting theories? Yes and no. Association theorists will retain their concern with past experiences, trials, practice, and so on, as the prime source of learning. They do, however, recognize the impact of situational factors on learning, especially outside the laboratory. At the same time, Koffka recognized the influence of past events on present learning: "The problem is best approached via memory, in which the past is represented somehow in the present." This influence enters through a rather elaborate *trace theory,* which incorporates past events (through memory) into present situations through a selective process which results in a new process of recall or recognition.[8]

A compromise between these opposing views of learning has not reached the consumer researcher. All research in the area appears to rely on the association (S-R) theories or their later mathematical representations, although a field-theoretical approach to consumer behavior has been proposed.[9]

The Learning Process

For the reason cited above, the following discussion leans primarily on the developments of the S-R school, specifically on reinforcement theory. We will ignore classical conditioning, which is concerned

[6] Hilgard and Bower, *Theories of Learning,* p. 229. Reference here is to Kurt Koffka, *The Growth of the Mind,* trans. R. M. Ogden (London: Kegan Paul, Trench, Trubner and Co., Ltd., 1924); and Wolfgang Köhler, *The Mentality of Apes,* trans. E. Winter (New York: Harcourt, Brace & World, 1925).

[7] Hilgard and Bower, *Theories of Learning,* p. 231.

[8] Hilgard and Bower, *Theories of Learning,* pp. 236-37.

[9] Harold H. Kassarjian, "Consumer Behavior: A Field Theoretical Approach," in *Marketing and the New Science of Marketing,* ed., Robert L. King (Chicago: American Marketing Association, 1968), pp. 285-89.

with the learning of reflex responses rooted primarily in physiological determinants. Our focus instead will be on *operant conditioning*, which deals with *voluntary* responses and is based on both physiological and learned needs or motives. We do this because of the much greater applicability of the latter to consumer behavior. The following description of an experiment illustrates much of the essence of operant conditioning, or voluntary learning.

> This time our subject is a little girl, about 17 months old, and the experimental situation is an ordinary livingroom, modified slightly to serve a laboratory purpose. Our observations begin as the little girl runs into the livingroom from the hallway and attempts to engage the attention of her mother, who sits by the window reading. Failing in her efforts, the child turns away. As her eyes wander over the room, they suddenly alight upon a new feature. Through a narrow gap between the sliding doors to the diningroom, a small, T-shaped handle projects itself. Just beneath the handle is a tin dish, easily within the child's reach. Approaching these objects quickly, but warily, the child touches the handle with her finger, and looks into the dish. As she does so, a small pellet of chocolate drops into the dish from a tube the other end of which is out of sight in the diningroom. Startled by this, the little girl momentarily withdraws from the dish, but returns to pick up the pellet and eat it. A few seconds later, she grasps the bar firmly and pulls it downward an inch or so, causing a second pellet to be discharged into the dish. From this time on, with rapidly growing efficiency, she operates the lever mechanism, eating each pellet as it comes, until the chocolate finally loses its appeal.[10]

Involved in that short description are several of the key elements in the learning process with which we shall deal, including the roles of drives and of reinforcement, and the associated processes of extinction, generalization, and discrimination.

ROLE OF DRIVES

The role of drives, or motives or needs,[11] in the learning process is generally accepted and plays a central role in the most elaborate S-R theory, that of Clark Hull.[12] We have devoted a large portion of Chapter 5 to the discussion of motivation, but some elementary notions will be useful here. *Motives* are the driving force behind all behavior, encompassing the body's most basic needs, such as hunger, thirst, and sex, and the higher social or learned needs, such as affection, status, and achievement.

Learning takes place because the response has satisfied some need. Let

[10] Fred S. Keller, *Learning: Reinforcement Theory* (New York: Random House, 1954), p. 6.

[11] Many psychologists insist on distinguishing among drives, motives, and needs. At times this is productive, at others, like now, it is counterproductive.

[12] For a summary of Hull's theory, see Hilgard and Bower, *Theories of Learning*, pp. 146-90.

us assume for a moment that chocolate pellets satisfy only the hunger need. The reason the little girl learned to pull that handle was because the pellet, when eaten, satisfied a drive—in this case, for food. Many psychological studies have dealt with the effect of drive strength on learning. By varying the level of deprivation, we find differences in the rate of learning. Had our little girl just polished off a large dish of chocolate ice cream and a piece of chocolate cake, we would expect the observed speed with which she "learned" the appropriate response to be slower. On the other hand, had some cruel experimenter forced her to go without food for 24 hours, the rate would have been faster—and would have lasted longer, i.e., until the drive level had been reduced. (For an example of how levels of food deprivation influence the amount of food purchased in a supermarket, see page 61 below.)

One of the factors which complicates the study of consumer behavior is evident in our little girl. We have only *assumed* hunger was the sole drive behind her lever-pulling behavior. It is likely that other motives, such as curiosity, "doing something prohibited," the need to remove boredom, or revenge against a mother who was ignoring her, were also present. Otherwise, countless tummyaches in children—and obesity in their parents—could have been prevented. The purchase of something as simple as a shampoo is likely to involve a complex set of needs—cleanliness, convenience, health, and perhaps sex ("It makes your hair more manageable than he'll ever be."). In learning terms, which drives are dominant? Which have been positively reinforced? Which are strengthening and which weakening repeat purchases? All these questions, and more, might face the consumer researcher concerned with the purchase and use of shampoos.

ROLE OF REINFORCEMENT

Positive reinforcement occurs when the individual experiences a reduction in the strength of a drive, such as the reduction of hunger in our little girl. Much of the research with animals involves this kind of positive reinforcement, or reward. When the reward is food for a hungry rat, water for a thirsty one, and so on, the researcher is using *primary* reinforcers. Much research, however, especially with human beings, involves *secondary* positive reinforcers. Examples of secondary reinforcing stimuli are showing approval with such words or acts as "good," "fine," "mmm-mmm," a head nod, or a smile when the subject gives a correct response.[13] A housewife may experience primary reinforcement after eating a delicious chocolate cake she had made from a Duncan–Hines mix. If her husband and children compliment her on her cooking, she is likely to experience an even stronger secondary reinforcement. Whether or not she purchases Duncan–Hines again is likely to be more a function of the latter than of

---

[13] Bernard Berelson and Gary A. Steiner, *Human Behavior: An Inventory of Scientific Findings* (New York: Harcourt, Brace & World, Inc., 1964), p. 144.

the former. This difference is even more pronounced in comparing the primary reinforcement she receives from the protection a new hat gives her from the sun, and the secondary reinforcement she receives from the envy of the other members of her bridge group. We will see in Chapter 7 how important primary groups can be in handing out reinforcement—both positive and negative.

EXTINCTION

Now suppose the housewife thought her cake was delicious, but the rest of the family quit eating after one or two bites; or that the hat she liked so much went unnoticed, or uncomplimented, by her bridge group. She has experienced positive primary reinforcement, but negative secondary reinforcement. In learning research, negative reinforcers, such as a head shake or an "uh-uh," are used to punish wrong responses in human subjects, as are electrical shocks or slaps on rats and other animals. It should be obvious what effect an electric shock (primary negative reinforcer) or a "no-no" (secondary negative reinforcer) instead of a piece of chocolate would have on the lever-pulling behavior of our little girl.

"Psychologists are often asked how to get rid of an already-conditioned behavior, how to *unlearn*, or how to learn *not* to do something . . . the basic formula is simple enough: *the way to unlearn an already-conditioned response is through 'extinction'—through the withholding of reinforcement.*" [14] When one of the authors was a young boy, he had a habit of biting his fingernails. This habit had no doubt been *learned* because the process had been reinforcing, perhaps through the reduction of an unknown (or not remembered) tension or drive. His mother was very anxious that he *unlearn* this behavior, and first tried a primary negative reinforcer—applying to his nails a foul-tasting but nontoxic liquid specifically designed for use on nail-biters and thumb-suckers. Individuals are often quite resistant to the extinction of some learned responses, and the nail-biter resisted these first attempts. Then his mother made him wear tape over his fingertips, and the ridicule of his peers (secondary negative reinforcer) finally caused extinction. Most psychological research indicates that extinction is indeed difficult to accomplish. We know of no specific research on extinction of consumer behavior (such as brand choice) under conditions of negative reinforcement; it is likely, however, that it can occur with less difficulty than appears in many of the laboratory settings.

GENERALIZATION

The principle of *generalization* in learning is quite simple, but it has some interesting implications for the student of consumer behavior. It states

[14] Keller, *Learning: Reinforcement Theory,* p. 8.

that we tend to respond to a new situation the way we did to similar past situations; that is, we generalize the learned S-R connection into new stimulus situations.

In his work with the conditioned response of salivation in dogs, Pavlov utilized a 1,000-cycle tone to condition the dog to salivate at the tone. He then exposed it to a number of other tones which, without exception, caused the dog to salivate, although always to a *lesser degree.* "Tones that were near in frequency to the conditioned stimulus produced, in general, more salivary flow than tones that were further away on the frequency scale." [15] In a later chapter (see pages 84–88), we shall see how the individual strives for cognitive balance or consistency. One mechanism for achieving this consistency is to generalize from one situation to similar ones. If our little girl encounters another lever in the room, she is likely to pull it and expect to get a piece of chocolate or some other goody. If the new lever is the same size and color as the first, she will be more likely to generalize than if the size, color, or both, have been changed.

Consumers display generalization when, after receiving shoddy service in the men's clothing department of a store, they expect shoddy service from other departments. If our housewife received strong positive reinforcement from her Duncan–Hines chocolate cake mix, she is likely to anticipate positive response to her use of a Duncan–Hines angel food cake mix. If a consumer has had poor performance from her General Electric toaster, she is likely to generalize that experience to General Electric irons.[16] If her husband has been well pleased with the two or three Chevrolets (a General Motors car) he has owned, he might strongly favor Oldsmobile (also a GM car) over Mercury or Dodge when he is able to buy a more expensive car.

Marketing managers have long been aware of the principle of generalization on the part of consumers. One policy decision facing firms with a number of products is over the use of "family brands," such as Betty Crocker cake mixes and Heinz "57 varieties." It is presumed that the consumer's experience (good or bad) with one of the products will be carried over, or *generalized,* to other products in the line. Procter and Gamble on the other hand, does little to associate their products. A consumer using Bold detergent, for instance, is not likely to be aware that the same company makes Cheer, Tide, and Oxydol. She is equally unlikely to know that the same company makes Jif peanut butter.[17]

---

[15] Keller, *Learning: Reinforcement Theory,* p. 14.

[16] Care must be exercised in regard to this principle, however, as many other factors might enter into the evaluation. Cf. Joe Kent Kerby, "Semantic Generalization in the Formation of Consumer Attitudes," *Journal of Marketing Research,* Vol. IV (August, 1967), 314-17.

[17] For a discussion of this common marketing problem, see E. Jerome McCarthy, *Basic Marketing: A Managerial Approach* (4th ed.) (Homewood, Ill.: Richard D. Irwin, Inc., 1971), pp. 292-94; or William J. Stanton, *Fundamentals of Marketing* (3rd ed.) (New York: McGraw-Hill Book Company, 1971), pp. 247-48.

DISCRIMINATION

Our common sense tells us that not all generalizations are appropriate. If we can use the independent tests of Consumers' Union as a guide, General Electric is capable of producing some small appliances which are highly recommended, even "excellent," and others which are "unacceptable." Experiences teach us to *discriminate* among stimuli which have previously been the subject of generalization.

Laboratory research in discrimination makes use of a supplementary stimulus. "The standard lever-pressing experiment may serve the purposes of discriminatory conditioning if the lever-pressing delivers a pellet of food in the presence of a positive, supporting stimulus (e.g., a 3 candlepower light) and fails to deliver in the absence of this discriminative stimulus." [18] We mentioned earlier that our little girl is likely to pull other levers she finds in the room, even if they are of different sizes and colors. If this generalization were not supported, she would learn to discriminate among levers, causing an extinction of the generalized learning. Suppose only red lever-pulling results in her getting a piece of chocolate: she soon *unlearns* the generalization that pulling all levers is an appropriate response. Similarly, if our housewife's angel food cake was a disappointment to her or brought forth negative reactions from her family, she might unlearn the generalization she made from Duncan–Hines chocolate cake mix to all mixes of that brand. The typical consumer has an extremely complex set of brand preferences which he has learned through considerable experience. Much of that learning has involved the discrimination among many brands of many product classes.

Learning in Consumer Behavior

When modern students of consumer behavior turned from the economic model, learning theory was one of the first places in which they sought more tenable alternative concepts. This was a logical move for two reasons: first, because of the relative sophistication of the theory and the abundance of research; and second, because learning is close to the central interests of many of those concerned with consumer behavior, primarily the scholar and practitioners in marketing and advertising.

[18] From the discussion of the operant conditioning theory of B. F. Skinner in Hilgard and Bower, *Theories of Learning*, p. 125.

THEORETICAL CONTRIBUTIONS TO CONSUMER BEHAVIOR [19]

From its first crude exposition by Howard in 1963 [20] to its final publication by Howard and Sheth in 1969,[21] *the theory of buyer behavior,* outlined in Chapter 1, has been primarily a learning model, rooted fairly firmly in the association or S-R theories of Spence, Hull, and Skinner. The model's construct *satisfaction* is defined in terms almost identical to Thorndike's Law of Effect.

> If the actual outcomes [of the purchase] are adjudged by the buyer to be *at least* equal to those expected, the buyer will feel satisfied, that is, actual consequences are greater than or equal to expected consequences. If, on the other hand, he adjudges the actual outcomes to be less than what he expected, the buyer will feel dissatisfied, that is actual consequences are less than expected consequences. . . . If the brand proves more satisfactory than he expected, the buyer has a tendency to enhance the attractiveness of the brand. If it proves less satisfactory than he expected, he is likely to diminish its attractiveness.[22]

There is, however, some link to the cognitive learning theories in that Howard and Sheth postulate that the level of satisfaction affects the consumer's attitudes and his choice criteria. They are also congruent with learning theory in their recognition that the level of satisfaction is the same as the "amount of reinforcement, measured indirectly by the reduction of the intensity of the Motives." [23]

A major postulate of the theory is that individuals learn brand choice through experience, based on what they call the *psychology of simplification.* The traditional learning curve is divided, as in Figure 3-1, into three periods. When the buyer is just beginning to purchase a product class, he actively seeks information—he has no narrowly defined set of alternatives. He is engaging more in *generalization* from previous experience than in *discrimination* among brands. This *extensive problem solving* (EPS) stage is followed by a stage of *limited problem solving* (LPS) where the buyer has more experience, engages in less information seeking behavior, and has begun discriminating so that he has a narrower

---

[19] In addition to the contributions reported here, the work of mathematical learning theorists has led to the development of stochastic, or probabilistic, models of buying behavior. Such models have been used to monitor market changes, to evaluate special promotions, and to monitor the introduction of new products. While space limitations prohibit presentation here, the interested student should see William F. Massy, David B. Montgomery, and Donald G. Morrison, *Stochastic Models of Buying Behavior* (Cambridge, Mass.: The M.I.T. Press, 1970).

[20] John A. Howard, *Marketing Management: Analysis and Planning* (rev. ed.) (Homewood, Ill.: Richard D. Irwin, Inc., 1963), Chs. 3 and 4.

[21] John A. Howard and Jagdish N. Sheth, *The Theory of Buyer Behavior* (New York: John Wiley & Sons, Inc., 1969).

[22] Howard and Sheth, *The Theory of Buyer Behavior,* p. 36.

[23] Howard and Sheth, *The Theory of Buyer Behavior,* p. 146. Much of this discussion is based on Howard and Sheth, pp. 145-50.

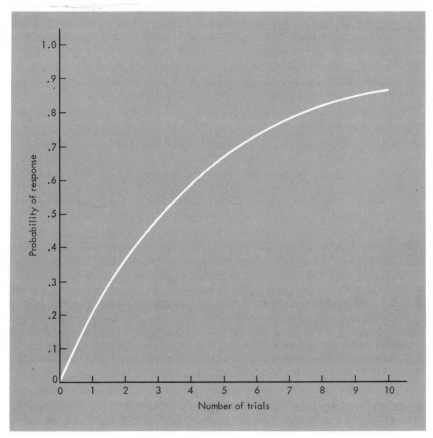

FIG. 3-1   The Learning Curve for Brand A

set of alternatives along with higher probabilities of choosing each one. In the final stage of *routinized response behavior* (RRB), the consumer has reached the point of habitually choosing a particular brand (so that the probability approaches 1.0) and engages in little, if any, information search.

Parts of this postulate have been tested. Utilizing the purchase of new automobiles, Bennett and Mandell found strong evidence for the contention that information-seeking behavior is reduced as the consumer "learns" brand choice through repetitive purchases of the brand.[24] In a laboratory setting, Sheth and Venkatesan found that subjects spent less time on information seeking as their repeat purchases increased.[25] There

[24] Peter D. Bennett and Robert M. Mandell, "Prepurchase Information Seeking Behavior of New Car Purchasers—The Learning Hypothesis," *Journal of Marketing Research*, Vol. VI (November, 1969), 430-33.

[25] Jagdish N. Sheth and M. Venkatesan, "Risk-Reduction Processes in Repetitive Consumer Behavior," *Journal of Marketing Research*, Vol. V (August, 1968), 307-10.

is fairly strong evidence (to be discussed more fully below) to support the other contention, that the probability of purchasing a brand increases as the number of past purchases of that brand increases.

ADVERTISING EFFECT

Advertisers have spent and continue to spend billions of dollars each year to convey selling messages to potential consumers. There is a firm belief that advertising does affect sales and profits in a positive way, or the practice would have ceased long ago. Yet, one of the most persistent problems advertisers face is specifying the effects of advertising on consumer behavior.

It is not appropriate to dwell on the entire complex issue here, but it is possible to discuss one major issue for which learning theory has meaning: the effect of repetitions of a stimulus (the ad) on the individual's ability to recall the message. Figure 3-2 compares the recall rates at four time periods for subjects who had heard one, two, four, and eight repe-

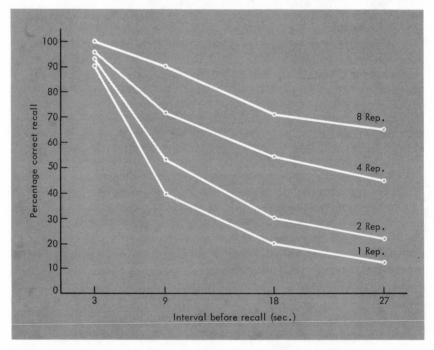

FIG. 3-2. Percentage of Correct Recalls as a Function of the Duration of Retention Interval Filled with Counting Backwards

The curves differ according to the number of consecutive presentations of the target item before the retention interval begins.

titions of a message.[26] While there was a decay in recall (forgetting) for all four conditions, the number of repetitions clearly affects learning positively. In a study of long-term decay in recall the effects of repetitions are similar. Figure 3-3 illustrates the recall over a one-year period of ad-

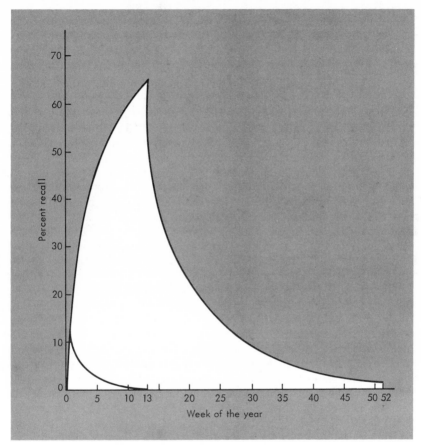

FIG. 3-3.   Recall of Advertising after One Exposure and after Thirteen Exposures

vertisements sent through the mail.[27] Both of these studies tend to support the position that advertising must be continuous to stop its being forgotten (it must be remembered, however, that these studies apply to the recall of specific messages).

[26] S. Hellyer, "Supplementary Report: Frequency of Stimulus Presentation and Short-term Decrement in Recall," *Journal of Experimental Psychology*, Vol. 64 (December, 1962), 650.
[27] Hubert A. Zielske, "The Remembering and Forgetting of Advertising," *Journal of Marketing*, Vol. 23 (January, 1959), 239-43.

BRAND LOYALTY

For centuries the loyalty of consumers toward a particular brand of a product has been of interest to marketing people since from their viewpoint it is a consummation devoutly to be wished. Brand loyalty has also been the topic of empirical research for the past 20 years.

In a series of articles in 1952, Brown reported on his analysis of 100 households in the *Chicago Tribune* consumer panel.[28] He identified four categories of consuming households. At one extreme was the household exhibiting "undivided loyalty," as when their purchases were in the brand sequence **AAAAA**. At the other extreme is the household showing "no loyalty," with a purchase sequence of **ABCDEF**. He included a category called "divided loyalty," as where a purchase sequence ran **ABABAB**. In many cases, one might argue that this is "undivided loyalty" to two noncompeting brands. In many homes, for instance, parents purchase one brand of toothpaste for themselves (for taste) and another for the children (for decay-preventatives). The fourth category of households were those with "unstable loyalty," as when a purchase sequence appeared like **AAABBB**. Again the interpretation is difficult; if the data were available, we might find that the string of purchase of Brand *A* stretches years into the past and of *B* for years into the future. That would indicate "undivided loyalty" with only one shift, making it a quite different behavior from a longer sequence like **AAABBBCCCDDD**.

Others examining brand loyalty have defined the phenomenon in terms of the proportion of purchases devoted to the most popular brand,[29] or on the length of a run of the same brand, on the number of runs in a sequence of a certain length,[30] or on the consistency of the most-favored brand over periods as long as 20 years.[31] It should be clear that all these attempts at defining brand loyalty are behavioral, that is, they define loyalty on the basis of what brands consumers actually buy. The popular meaning of the word "loyalty" is more likely to evoke a definition related to emotional allegiance, such as "loyalty to one's country." This would indicate that brand loyalty has an *affective* or *cognitive* dimension of which the behavioral dimension is a result.

You will recall that one of the major questions about learning is, "What is learned, habits or cognitive structures?" You will also recall that the answer was a major source of difference between association and cog-

[28] George Brown, "Brand Loyalty—Fact or Fiction?" *Advertising Age*, Vol. 23 (9 issues between June 19, 1952, and January 26, 1953).

[29] Ross Cunningham, "Brand Loyalty—What, Where, How Much," *Harvard Business Review*, Vol. 34 (January-February, 1956), 116-28; and Ronald E. Frank, "Is Brand Loyalty a Useful Basis for Market Segmentation?" *Journal of Advertising Research*, Vol. 7 (June, 1967), 27-33.

[30] Jagdish N. Sheth, "How Adults Learn Brand Preference," *Journal of Advertising Research*, Vol. 8 (September, 1968), 25-36.

[31] Lester Guest, "Brand Loyalty Revisited: A Twenty-Year Report," *Journal of Applied Psychology*, Vol. 48 (April, 1964), 93-97.

nitive theorists. Without repeating the arguments, it appears that the association theorists have done more explaining of brand loyalty, with the result that it has become synonymous with habit.

But they have not been responsible for quite all of it. An important study by Krugman and Hartley on the "learning of tastes" deals more directly with cognitive and affective components, that is, familiarity with and liking for objects.[32] Tucker has long contended that it is possible to separate the process of developing brand loyalty from the strength of the loyalty once developed. In an experimental study, he described the former in behavioral terms, as have others,[33] but he tested the cognitive or affective dimensions by supplying increasing levels of incentive to the subjects to break their loyalty.

Finally, some recent research into brand loyalty has focused directly on the question of loyalty as *cognitive commitment*. The work is based on the recent development in attitudes by the Sherifs,[34] who argue that an attitude cannot accurately be captured by one point on a scale from very negative to very positive. Rather, there are acceptable positions on both sides of the point that the individual finds *most* acceptable on an attitude scale. These they would put into his "latitude of acceptance."

In terms of brands of a product, a person might have a most preferred brand, but other brands may also fall into his *latitude of acceptance* (A). Other brands, through negative experience, or perhaps through the influence of other persons, have been rejected, i.e., are in the *latitude of rejection* (R). Still others fall into the *latitude of noncommitment* (NC), which includes brands that, for one reason or another, have been neither accepted nor rejected.

Using these categories, Jacoby and Olson have defined brand commitment (brand loyalty) as a simple ratio between the latitudes of acceptance and rejection, R/A, ignoring the latitude of noncommitment.[35] This formulation is not strictly in keeping with the Sherifs' work, which says that the more involved and personally committed the individual is, the greater is the latitude of rejection in relation to the latitude of acceptance, the number of positions on which he remains noncommittal approaching zero.

A more recent formulation, and one consistent with the Sherifs', is being tested in two doctoral dissertations under the supervision of one of

[32] Herbert E. Krugman and Eugene L. Hartley, "The Learning of Tastes," *The Public Opinion Quarterly*, Vol. 24 (Winter, 1960), 621-31.

[33] W. T. Tucker, "The Development of Brand Loyalty," *Journal of Marketing Research*, Vol. 1 (August, 1964), 32-35.

[34] Cf. Carolyn W. Sherif, Muzafer Sherif, and R. E. Nebergall, *Attitude and Attitude Change: The Social Judgment-Involvement Approach* (Philadelphia: W. B. Saunders Co., 1965); and Muzafer Sherif and Carl I. Hovland, *Social Judgment: Assimilation and Contrast Effects in Communication and Attitude Change* (New Haven, Conn.: Yale University Press, 1961).

[35] Jacob Jacoby and Jerry C. Olson, "An Attitudinal Model of Brand Loyalty: Conceptual Underpinnings and Instrumentation Research" (Unpublished paper presented at the University of Illinois Conference on Attitude Research and Consumer Behavior, December, 1970). In this paper they actually reverse the ratio, A/R, giving an inverse measure of loyalty.

the authors.[36] That definition retains the ratio of Jacoby and Olson, but also includes the effect of the latitude of noncommitment. Algebraically, it appears as

$$\text{brand loyalty} = \frac{R}{A} (1.0 - NC),$$

where all latitudes are expressed as proportions of the total. Note that as the consumer accepts fewer brands, relative to the number he rejects, he becomes more loyal, and as the number to which he is noncommitted declines, the loyalty level increases.

Preliminary results indicate that the approach is quite promising. There are some very important theoretical and practical implications of this new research. First, it will have established the cognitive/affective dimension of brand loyalty. Second, and perhaps most important, it will have developed an empirical measure of brand loyalty which does not depend on the extremely costly and time-consuming panel method of data collection. Brand loyalty has long been a useful concept in the study of consumer behavior and promises to become even more useful in the future.

Summary

1. Definitions of learning, in a technical sense, must include aspects of (a) more or less permanent change in behavior which occurs as a result of practice, and (b) the process by which an activity originates or is changed through reacting to an encountered situation.

2. Learning theorists differ over *what* we learn. The S-R school says we learn habits, or links between stimulus and response (because of reinforcement, or through contiguity in time), while the *cognitive* school says that we learn cognitive structures.

3. *How* we learn is either through *trial and error* (S-R school), or through *insight* (*Gestalt* school). The student of consumer behavior should be open to contributions from various schools of thought, since both *what* we learn and *how* we learn it probably differ in different market situations.

4. Learning takes place because the response has satisfied some need or needs, thus the roles of drives, motives, or needs cannot be overlooked. We should be especially aware of the possibility that the purchase of a product (such as a shampoo) may be associated with a number of needs (other than cleanliness).

5. *Reinforcement* is probably involved in the learning of preferences for products; it may be *primary* (as when a housewife is satisfied with a cake she has baked) or *secondary* (as when her husband and children compliment her on it).

6. *Extinction* of learning, as when a consumer shifts away from a favor-

---

[36] Andres San Agustin, "An Investigation of Brand Commitment, Confidence, and Attitude in the Theory of Buyer Behavior," and Lance P. Jarvis, "Product Class Importance and Brand Commitment as Mediators in Consumer Brand Choice Behavior."

ite brand, may occur as a result of negative reinforcement, although research in consumer behavior is scant here.

7. *Generalization,* learning to respond in a new situation as we have learned to do in similar situations, is of interest to marketing. It is involved in how a consumer will react to other products of the same make (if Duncan–Hines chocolate cake mix is good, then so must its angel food cake mix), and thus in the decision of whether or not to follow a policy of "family brands."

8. Conversely, *discriminations* are learned when through experience we learn that not all generalizations are valid. A consumer's learned preferences are typically quite complex—he may think that a G.E. toaster is excellent but that Motorola's TV set is vastly superior to that of G.E.

9. In addition to the theoretical contributions of learning, it has been applied to the study of the *effectiveness of advertising,* especially to the impact of repetition in advertising.

10. Learning theory has been applied to the study of how consumers learn *brand loyalty.* Early research dealt primarily with the behavioral dimensions of loyalty, while recent efforts have been concerned with the affective and cognitive dimensions.

4

PERCEPTION

The behavior of the consumer in the marketplace depends to a large extent on his knowledge of the world about him. In times of food shortage he may hoard flour, sugar, and oil. During a recession he tends to tighten up on his spending, especially for frivolous items, while during runaway inflation he spends his money as quickly as it is earned. What we "know" about the world around us comes from our perceptions. Sensory inputs such as light, sound, pressure, and odors must be perceived and cognitively organized into meaningful patterns before they can be acted upon. Sensations from the outside world are altered by previous learning, memories, expectations, fantasies, beliefs, attitudes, values, and personality beyond the pure stimulus. The integration of these perceptions, memories, expectations, beliefs, and attitudes, and so forth, comprises the individual's cognitive structure.

Sensation independent of perception probably does not exist. We do not hear combinations of notes at fixed frequencies; we hear music, we hear a baby crying, we hear an instructor professing. We perceive not random sensations but rather organized and meaningful percepts; very few percepts exist alone. Seeing a stranger drive on campus in a Mercedes-Benz means more than a man driving a vehicle. More than transportation is expressed; we see elegance, wealth, sophistication, urbanity. It may imply a university patron, a "fat cat," the establishment, but not merely rubber, steel, paint, and glass. But suppose that the driver is black. The most likely expectation is that he is a chauffeur. But suppose further that he is dressed shoddily and the back seat contains a poorly-dressed child who has left layers of ice cream stains on the upholstery. Once again our cognitive structures allow for a meaningful organization or interpretation. We are not overwhelmed by random sensations, but as more information is available our cognitions are reorganized from one meaningful structure to another.

Hence, the perceptions of the individual are selectively organized. He perceives objects, products, people, not electrical impulses from nerve fibers. Furthermore, only certain objects in the geographic world enter into his cognitions. Others are not perceived, and those characteristics that are perceived are molded or altered to fit the requirements of the individual.[1] The determinants of perception, the principles of cognitive organization, are grouped by most scholars into two major categories, *stimulus* factors and *functional* factors.

STIMULUS FACTORS

These factors are derived solely from the nature of the physical stimuli and the neutral effects they evoke in the nervous system of the individual. To the Gestalt psychologists discussed in the previous chapter, perceptual organizations are determined primarily by the physiological events occurring in the nervous system of the individual in direct reaction to stimulation by the physical objects.[2] This approach does not deny the importance of needs, moods, and expectations in the perceptual process, but rather emphasizes physical characteristics such as size, color, surroundings, movement, and contrast. For example, a color ad in a newspaper will be noticed by a larger percentage of readers than will the same ad in black and white, merely due to the contrast of color among pages of black print.

Similarity. One of the major stimulus factors of organization is similarity. Other things being equal, similar things tend to be perceived as belonging together: for instance, all students with beards and long hair may be perceived as radical revolutionaries about to destroy property; bankers tend to be grouped with capitalist warmongers who put property rights before human rights. A simple diagram may clarify the principle of similarity. Most individuals, when asked what they see in Figure 4-1,

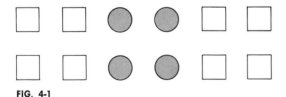

FIG. 4-1

respond with two sets of four white squares and one set of four black dots. Seldom will people see two horizontal lines, each line consisting of squares and dots.

Proximity. Other things being equal, things near each other tend to be perceived as belonging together. In Figure 4-2 the usual perception

[1] David Krech, Richard S. Crutchfield, and Egerton L. Ballachey, *Individual in Society* (New York: McGraw-Hill Book Co., 1962), p. 20.
[2] David Krech and Richard S. Crutchfield, *Theory and Problems of Social Psychology* (New York: McGraw-Hill Book Co., 1948), p. 81.

FIG. 4-2

is three columns of four dots rather than four rows of three dots. Guilt by association, by proximity, was one of the horrors of the McCarthy era. Robert J. Oppenheimer, the developer of the Atomic Bomb during World War II's super-secret Manhattan Project, some years afterward had his security clearance revoked by President Eisenhower because he and his wife allegedly had acquaintances who were suspected of being communists.

In New York a man recently died of botulism poisoning in a can of Bon Vivant vichyssoise. Consumers found all that company's products "guilty" by association, and the company was forced to declare bankruptcy. Campbell Soup later encountered a contamination scare, with all its soups "suspect," and the company lost an estimated $10,000,000 in sales.[3]

Continuity. Stimuli that form a complete or symmetrical figure, or good form, tend to be grouped as part of a whole. Figure 4-3 is usually per-

FIG. 4-3

ceived as a hexagonal object rather than three rows of two dots each. In fact, our need for good form is so great that we may even supply elements in order to achieve closure, to perceive a meaningful whole. The producers of Salem cigarettes have used this principle rather successfully by constant repetition of the jingle:

> You can take Salem out of the country,
> But you can't take the country out of Salem.

Once the advertisers felt that the audience could hum this jingle to the point of near exasperation, they changed it to:

> You can take Salem out of the country, but. . . .

[3] "These Products Made News in 1971," *Advertising Age,* Vol. 43 (January 3, 1972), p. 45.

Because the jingle did not have good form (closure), most listeners felt compelled to complete the sentence and the tune to themselves. Presumably the advertisers feel it will help sales if people are compelled to hum quietly to themselves, "You can't take the country out of Salem."

Context. The context, the environment or the setting of an object, often determines how a thing will be perceived. A classic example found in most introductory psychology textbooks is the reversible figure and background illustration found in Figure 4-4: if the background is per-

FIG. 4-4

ceived as black, the figure is a vase or goblet; if the background is seen as white, the figure is two black profiles. Context is often a concern of advertisers. The influence of programming on the viewer's perception of commercials on television is a constant fear of advertisers; as a result, many claims of influence-peddling on program content are heard, apocryphal or not.

Fuchs conducted an interesting study on the influence of the context of an ad on attitudes toward the advertised product. Selecting two very little-known automotive products and creating similar ads, such that in one form a low-prestige manufacturer was "advertising" the item and in the other case a high-prestige manufacturer, he rather skillfully placed these ads artificially into a high-prestige magazine (one such as *Harpers, Atlantic,* or *New Yorker*) and into a low-prestige magazine (such as *True Detective, Male,* or *Confidential*). Subjects were asked to rate the quality and reputation of the product. As might be expected, the product placed in the high-prestige magazine was rated much higher than the same product in the same ad placed in the low-prestige magazine.[4]

Other Stimulus Factors. A host of still other stimulus characteristics are of interest to advertisers. Larger sizes normally produced more atten-

[4] Douglas A. Fuchs, "Two Source Effects in Magazine Advertising," *Journal of Marketing Research,* Vol. 1 (August, 1964), 59-62.

tion than smaller sizes; a large ad in a newspaper or magazine is noticed and read more often than a small ad, although the increase is not linear. Loud sounds and bright colors, especially if in a context of serenity, are more noticed than quiet colors or sounds; the packaging for detergents such as Bold, Drive, and Tide are examples of grotesque art work used as attention-getters. Movement is often perceived more easily than stationary objects; point-of-purchase displays, neon signs with moving arrows, rotating billboards, and animated signs are such examples. However, man has great ability to adapt to pain, odors, warmth, and cold, and to sounds, bright colors, neon signs, and movement. Hence contrast itself aids perception. Although on a semiclassical music radio station loudly squealing tires will probably attract our attention, this is not necessarily so on a frantic rock station. In these conditions silence and a soft-spoken voice are often more noticeable.

One final stimulus characteristic is that of optical or geometrical illusions. For example, in Figure 4-5 distances *ab* and *bc* are identical, as are

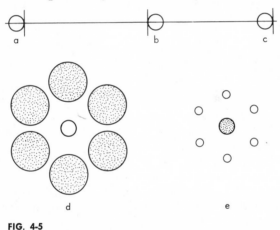

FIG. 4-5

the diameters of the inner circles *d* and *e*, although visually this would not seem true. One can only speculate how often package shapes and designs are specifically created to give an illusion of being larger than they actually are.

Sensory Thresholds. If we are presented with two sounds, one of 3,000 cycles per second and another at 3,005 cycles per second, we cannot perceive the difference, nor can we generally perceive sounds below 30 or 40 cycles or above 15,000 cycles per second. Thirty-cycle sounds are below our lower threshold of sensation, while 15,000-cycle sounds are above our upper threshold, although in some animals—dogs, for example—the upper threshold is considerably higher. All creatures have an increment threshold. That point at which we can just notice differences is called a *j.n.d.* (just noticeable difference); a difference just below the j.n.d. is called *j.n.n.d.* (just not-noticeable difference). Weber in the 1800's developed a mathematical formula on the relationship of the j.n.d.

to the original stimulus itself. Now termed the Weber-Fechner law, the formula, which holds well for the middle ranges of intensities of stimuli but not for either extreme, is:

$$\frac{\Delta I}{I} = K$$

where

ΔI is the smallest increase in intensity to be noticed (j.n.d.),
I is the original intensity, and
K is the constant that varies from one sense modality to another.

In other words, the stronger the initial intensity, the greater the increment necessary to produce a perceptible difference. The amount of salt it takes to make potato chips taste just slightly more salty (j.n.d.) depends on how much salt was used in the first place. Whereas experimental evidence backs up Weber's law in such sensory processes as sound, light, smell, taste, pressure, pain, and so on, it is merely speculation whether such constants would emerge in price, product design, preference, or other aspects of consumer behavior outside of sensory processes. Perhaps the perception of the number of dollars that the price of a refrigerator should fall below a competitor's price in order to be noticed depends on the competitor's original price. And although $30 might be sufficient for a refrigerator, it is not sufficient for a $5,000 car, and far more than a j.n.d. for an electric toaster. (An excellent empirical study by Kamen and Toman refutes the Weber psychophysical relationship when applied to pricing; there is also a rejoinder to this study by Monroe.[5])

FUNCTIONAL FACTORS

Although in the perceptual process the importance of the physical stimulus must not be underestimated, there is much more to perception than merely a stimulus impinging on the neural receptors in the eye or ear. Perceptions do not occur in an unorganized state. We perceive only those things that make sense within the context of our cognitive structures. On one hand, we screen out messages we do not want to perceive; on the other, we distort, modify, and often add elements so that very often we see what we want to see.

Hastorf and Cantril present a fascinating example of the influence of functional factors in the viewing of a football game.[6] The football contest between two Ivy League teams, Princeton and Dartmouth, was unusually rough and emotionally charged; numerous injuries occurred, and

[5] See Joseph M. Kamen and Robert J. Toman, "Psychophysics of Price," *Journal of Marketing Research*, Vol. 7 (February, 1970), 27-35; and Kent B. Monroe, "Psychophysics of Price: A Reappraisal," *Journal of Marketing Research*, in press.
[6] Albert H. Hastorf and Hadley Cantril, "They Saw a Game: A Case History," *Journal of Abnormal and Social Psychology*, Vol. 49 (1954), 129-34.

the referees were kept busy blowing their whistles and penalizing both sides. The results of the study indicated that fault or blame of the troublesome tactics could be laid on either side, depending on which fans were questioned. The fans of these two teams, sitting in the same stadium on the same Saturday afternoon, saw two different games. Hastorf and Cantril conclude that no such thing as a "game," objectively observed, existed out there. Out of all the occurrences going on in the environment, each fan selected those that had some significance for him. In other words, reality, like beauty, is in the eyes of the beholder.

Another classic example of the functional aspects of perception is documented by the social effects of Upton Sinclair's best-selling novel, *The Jungle*. Sinclair was a socialist and an ardent supporter of the underpaid and overworked. He hated cruelty, he hated child labor, he hated employer tyranny and the blacklisting of men who tried to improve their lot by forming unions. He wrote a book about the indignant working and health conditions in the meat-packing industry: plants were filthy, and safety precautions were nonexistent—a man could lose an arm, a body, or an overly-friendly rat in the lard vats. The book became a best seller; it was translated into twenty-seven languages; and it led to reforms and federal laws and regulations in meat processing—*not* in labor protection, *not* in union regulations, *not* in safety standards, *not* in social welfare, but in the handling of meat. The constituency of legislators were not socialists; they did not see the plight of the oppressed worker—they saw the rat falling into a salami machine and becoming processed, packaged, and labeled.[7]

Attention. Of the multitude of physical energies surrounding us at any given moment of time, we can perceive only a few. In some cases, by virtue of the physical characteristics of the stimuli our sense organs tune them out. High frequency sound, low and high wavelengths of light, cosmic radiation, radioactivity, and electromagnetic waves are imperceptible without instruments like a radio receiver, Geiger counter, or such, to convert the energies into stimuli that we are capable of sensing.

As previously mentioned, some stimuli force us involuntarily to pay attention; contrast, movement, size, loud sounds and colors, the screech of chalk on the blackboard, and repetition are such examples. Among other gimmicks found on radio to draw attention to the commercial are such things as voice modulation, jingles, telephone rings, cattle stampedes, bells and gongs, static, police whistles, animal noises, clapping hands, trains and motors, screaming children, and finally the ultimate—silence.

Above and beyond these physical characteristics or stimulus factors, the interests of the perceiver aid him in *filtering out* some of the energies and focusing on others. Research has indicated that ads for golf balls attract considerable attention from the golfing enthusiast when placed in *Time*. However, the very same ads placed in *Golf Digest* will be missed by many golfers. The interests of the golfer, while he is thumbing through *Time*, focus his attention on an ad for golf balls. In the special interest

[7] As reported in Krech, *et al., Individual in Society,* pp. 23-24.

magazine, however, he is unable to pay equal attention to the entire spectrum of stimuli.[8]

Needs. The influence of physiological needs as a factor in perception has been clearly demonstrated in dozens of studies. For example, pictures of food flashed on a screen for very short periods of time were more readily recognized when subjects were hungry than when they were not hungry.[9] In a somewhat similar study [10] 189 incomplete words such as S___ ___AK, ___E___LY, were presented to twenty-six obese men who were to undergo a starvation diet. The researchers hypothesized that obese men would make more food-related responses than average people in completing the words after being deprived of food for a long time and that the relative frequency of food-related responses would increase as the length of deprivation increased. The results supported the hypotheses both for one-week and one-month intervals.

Psychological needs influence perception in a similar manner. The influence on perception of such needs as status, dominance, love affiliation, and so forth, are today so well accepted by scientist and layman alike that they need no further elaboration.

Preparatory Set. Some of the selectivity in perception is due to the expectation, or "set," the perceiver holds. This is a common problem among track runners lined up for an event; a cough, a movement, or a rustle is perceived as the starting gun and someone leaps forward. Bruner and Postman examined this factor by flashing pictures of playing cards before subjects for short periods. After a brief exposure the subjects were asked to identify the cards. Among the exposed cards were specially prepared ones, such as a black six of hearts or a red four of spades; twenty-seven of the twenty-eight subjects called the black four of hearts either a red four of hearts or a black four of spades. The set of prior experience distorted either the color or the shape of the stimuli.[11] It is estimated that as many as one-fourth of all ads are attributed to the wrong sponsor. The consumer once again apparently perceives what he expects to see.

Similar results are found in a tightly controlled pair of experiments by Makens. In the first experiment two samples of identical turkey meat were presented to subjects, one labeled with a well-known brand and the other labeled with an unknown brand. The well-known brand was preferred. In the second experiment subjects were presented with two samples of turkey meat, one much tougher (that is, less tender or possessing a greater shearing strength) than the other. Subjects were asked to state which they preferred and to identify the brand of each. As might be

[8] This is not to imply that *Time* is necessarily a better medium for golfing ads. Other variables must be considered.

[9] R. S. Lazarus, H. Yossem, and D. Arenberg, "Hunger and Perception," *Journal of Personality,* Vol. 21 (1953), 312-28.

[10] E. Crumpton, D. B. Wine, and E. J. Drenick, "Effects of Prolonged Food Deprivation on Food Responses to Skeleton Words," *Journal of General Psychology,* Vol. 76 (1967), 179-82.

[11] Jerome S. Bruner and Leo J. Postman, "On the Perception of Incongruity: A Paradigm," *Journal of Personality,* Vol. 18 (1949), 206-23.

expected, the more tender meat was preferred, and it was claimed that the preferred meat was taken from the well-known brand of turkey. Apparently a well-known brand is expected to be of superior quality than an unknown brand. Studies on cigarettes, cola beverages, and beer support these results. Subjects usually cannot perceive differences between brands in a blind test; however, if the labels are left on, clear preferences and quality evaluations emerge.[12]

Other variables. Numerous other studies, both in and out of the field of consumer behavior, indicate that an individual's values, attitudes, and beliefs, as well as his personality, influence the manner in which the world is organized and perceived. For example, the concept of *perceptual defense* has been well established. If subjects are presented with culturally or socially taboo words, words that violate his value system, such as rape, vagina, or intercourse, for a brief moment of time on a screen, they will have difficulty perceiving these words. Non-taboo or neutral words such as table, chair, and dog, are perceived much more easily. On the other hand, socially valued words and concepts are more rapidly perceived than are neutral words.[13]

The influence of political values on the perception of a candidate for an election can be found in a study by Kassarjian. A sample of 3,000 voters, after the third television debate between Kennedy and Nixon in 1960, were asked for whom they intended to vote. A number of questions later they were queried as to who the respondent thought was taller, Nixon or Kennedy. (It was assumed the presidency would be perceived as a big job requiring a big man.) The results indicated that Nixon voters felt Nixon was taller and Kennedy voters thought that Kennedy was taller.[14] Many other such examples of the relevance of one's frame of reference will become evident in the ensuing chapters.

If one projects to problems of international marketing, the work of Benjamin Lee Whorf in psycholinguistics becomes particularly important. Not only are personal values and tensions relevant to perception, but Whorf argues that the very language one speaks, the grammar, the lexical units influence how man habitually perceives the world about him. The world of a Hopi Indian or an Apache, a Chinese diplomat or African politician, is not the identical world of the individual who speaks an Indo-

[12] For example, see N. H. Pronko and D. T. Herman, "Identification of Cola Beverages: IV. Postscript," *Journal of Applied Psychology,* Vol. 46 (1962), 358-60; C. K. Raymond, L. N. Rachal, and M. R. Marks, "Brand Discrimination among Cigarette Smokers," *Journal of Applied Psychology,* Vol. 34 (1950), 282-84; and Ralph I. Allison and Kenneth P. Uhl, "Influence of Beer Brand Identification on Taste Perception," *Journal of Marketing Research,* Vol. 1 (August, 1964), 36-39.

[13] E. McGinnies, "Emotionality and Perceptual Defense," *Psychological Review,* Vol. 56 (1949), 244-51; Leo J. Postman, Jerome S. Bruner, and E. McGinnies, "Personal Values as Selective Factors in Perception," *Journal of Abnormal and Social Psychology,* Vol. 43 (April, 1948), 142-54.

[14] Harold H. Kassarjian, "Voting Intentions and Political Perception," *Journal of Psychology,* Vol. 56 (1963), 85-88.

European language such as English, French, Spanish, or Greek. That any international understanding exists at all is no less than amazing.[15]

Perceptual Mapping

Beginning very recently, some of the knowledge in perception from the field of psychology has been applied rather ingeniously to marketing problems by the use of complex computer technology. Volney Stefflre first introduced the technique to marketing with the claim that it can estimate the share of consumer choices that a new brand will receive when it is placed on the market, and further that it will estimate the patterns of substitution and competition that will exist after the new brand is introduced.

The psychological logic behind the methodology is quite simple and yet very powerful: "An individual will behave toward a new thing in a manner that is similar to the way he behaves toward other things he sees the new thing as being similar to." [16] In other words, as a new product or brand is introduced, the consumer will perceive it as being either similar or dissimilar to other existing brands on several dimensions. For example, if some product category consists of three brands, *A*, *B*, and *C*, and if we market a new brand, *X*, which consumers see as being similar to *B* but unlike *A* and *C*, then those consumers who previously bought *B* will be just as likely to buy *X* as *B*. Other things being equal (price, promotion, distribution, etc.), brand *B* will share its market with the new brand *X*, while the entry of *X* will not affect the market shares of *A* and *C*. This makes good sense since consumers perceive *X* and *B* as being quite similar to each other but both are perceived as quite dissimilar to *A* and *C*.[17]

Since products may be perceived to vary on several dimensions and, in fact, the consumers may not be consciously aware of the dimensions or the interactions of one variable with another, methodologies used in multidimensional scaling have been used both to identify the perceptual maps of consumers as well as to help in identifying and labeling the dimensions.

An example of a two-dimensional map is presented in Figure 4-6. The information collected from consumers might be *preference* data (Which of each of these pairs of beer do you prefer?), or *similarities* data (Among these beers taken three at a time, which two are most similar and which

[15] Benjamin Lee Whorf, *Language, Thought and Reality: Selected Writings of Benjamin Lee Whorf*, John B. Carroll, ed. (Cambridge, Mass.: The Technology Press of the Massachusetts Institute of Technology, and New York: John Wiley & Sons, Inc., 1956).

[16] Volney Stefflre, "Simulation of People's Behavior toward New Objects and Events," *American Behavioral Scientist*, Vol. 8 (May, 1965), 12-15.

[17] Alvin J. Silk, "Preference and Perception Measures in New Product Development: An Exposition and Review," *Industrial Management Review*, Vol. 11 (Fall, 1969), 21-37.

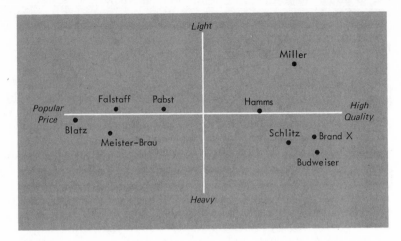

FIG. 4-6

Source: Richard M. Johnson, "Market Segmentation: A Strategic Management Tool," *Journal of Marketing Research*, Vol. 8 (February, 1971), 13-18.

two are least similar?). The computer programs will provide the geometric distances between brands in several dimensional spaces. It is then up to the researcher to place labels on the variables. In the example in Figure 4-6, the researcher chose to name his dimensions "popular price–high quality" and "light–heavy." If these data are accurate, we can assume that Brand X will compete with Schlitz and Budweiser and have much less competitive effect on Blatz and Miller.

The method is useful not only for new product opportunities but can be most useful in product and promotion strategies. It can help the seller determine whether consumers have a similar or dispersed image of his brand, aid him in knowing what the image of his brand is, and indicate how he may go about changing it if he wishes.[18]

Perceived Risk and Cognitive Processes

In recent years a great deal of excitement and research has been generated around the concept of perceived risk. Consumer behavior, that is, any action of the consumer, has the potential to produce consequences that cannot be anticipated with anything approximating certainty.[19] Any purchase competes with numerous alternative uses of the same financial resources; the product may not work properly; or the consumer may be criticized by others for the foolishness of his decision. For a large-ticket item such as a late-model used car, stocks, or the purchase of a home at

[18] Philip Kotler, *Marketing Decision Making: A Model Building Approach* (New York: Holt, Rinehart and Winston, 1971), pp. 491-97.

[19] Raymond A. Bauer, "Consumer Behavior as Risk Taking," in *Dynamic Marketing for a Changing World*, ed. Robert S. Hancock, Proceedings of the 43rd Conference of the American Marketing Association.

a time of high interest rates and a falling real estate market, the perception of risk can become quite uncomfortable. Cox theorizes that risk may often be perceived by the consumer as the result of one or more of the follcwing factors: [20]

1. *She may be uncertain as to what the buying goals are.* Would she rather have an outrageously expensive new cocktail dress or a new piece of furniture? If a dress, should it be the cocktail dress she has always wanted or a more functional wool suit?

2. *The consumer may be uncertain as to which purchase (product, brand, model, etc.) will best match or satisfy acceptance level of buying goals.* Should the suit be purchased at Lord and Taylor's or the local discount house? Will she really be more satisfied with a modern styling or a more conservative basic cut?

3. *The consumer may perceive possible adverse consequences if the purchase is made (or not made) and the result is a failure to satisfy her buying goals.* For example, she may suffer intense embarrassment if she buys her cocktail dress and it is much too risqué at a party, or she looks fat, or it fits poorly.

According to Cox, "If one or more of these conditions are present in the cognitions of the consumer, we would define the situation as one of perceived risk. In short, risk is a function of two elements, uncertainty and consequences." [21] The uncertainty relates to the buying goals; the consequences relate to the quality and performance of the product and the ability of the product to fulfill the psychological and social needs of the individual.

Although most buying situations are perceived as containing some risk, certainly the consumer more often than not is able to deal with it. Bruner and Tajfel classify consumers into two major coping styles: *the narrow categorizer,* who prefers the risk of reacting and possibly being wrong, and *the broad categorizer,* who prefers the risk of not reacting and possibly being wrong.[22] Women seem to be consistently more narrow in their categorizing than men. Young men are more confident in their judgments than older men, but there is no difference among women in this respect. Older subjects are less extreme than younger, suggesting that an important consequence of aging might be a greater unwillingness to "go out on a limb" even when one is highly confident of his judgment. The student who has studied statistics may appreciate that these coping styles are analogous to Type I and Type II errors in hypothesis testing.

Obviously, perceived risk is an individual variable; risk-taking does

[20] Donald F. Cox, ed., *Risk Taking and Information Handling in Consumer Behavior* (Boston: Division of Research, Graduate School of Business Administration, Harvard University, 1967), pp. 5-6.

[21] Cox, *Risk Taking and Information Handling in Consumer Behavior,* p. 6.

[22] Jerome S. Bruner and H. Tajfel, "Cognitive Risk and Environmental Change," *Journal of Abnormal and Social Psychology,* Vol. 62 (1961), 231-41.

not imply that consumers try to calculate probabilities and consequences as in the expected value concept in statistical decision theory. In fact, seldom does the individual act in mathematically rational terms in decision-making. Otherwise, he would probably never purchase insurance, place a bet on the gambling tables, purchase goods to enter contests, or visit the race track. Nevertheless, perhaps risk reduction is normal behavior in the marketplace, since the consumer generally tends to become brand loyal, has favorite restaurants, or purchases information at the race track.

Risk can be reduced either by decreasing the possible consequences or increasing the certainty of the possible outcome. One reads ads and *Consumer Reports*, examines the product, asks or looks to others—especially individuals who are perceived as experts or opinion leaders—sticks to the "tried and true," purchases national or advertised brands for assurance or quality or private labels to reduce the financial risk, or begins to expect less from the product, lowering his level of aspiration to protect himself from perceived failure in the purchase decision. Arndt has found that high-risk perceivers were more brand loyal, tended to avoid being among the first persons to try new products, switched brands less often, were more likely to seek information and more likely to respond to information they have sought (although later studies are not as clear).[23]

Obviously, then, perceivers both of high risk and of low risk use a cognitive style of coping with the world around them by organizing perceptions along with experiences, behavior, and lifestyle to make the world a more meaningful place in which to exist.

The Attribution Process

Not only do we perceive reality in line with our particular cognitive style, but we also tend to perceive causality, that is, to attribute an interrelationship when events occur in a chain. Thus, one individual "may attribute a caustic remark by an associate to that person's hostile personality, a pay raise to his own superior ability, and the birth of a son rather than a daughter to 'good luck.' Yet another person may attribute a male birth to a benevolent god in answer to his prayers or to the juxtaposition of the stars and his adherence to astrological forecasts."[24]

The attribution process was first described by Fritz Heider in his book, *The Psychology of Interpersonal Relations.*[25] He noted that man is not usually content simply to register the observables that surround him; he needs to relate them as far as possible to the invariances in his environment. Correct attributions always serve to build up and support the

[23] Johan Arndt, "Word of Mouth Advertising and Perceived Risk," in *Perspectives in Consumer Behavior*, Harold H. Kassarjian and Thomas S. Robertson, eds. (Glenview, Ill.: Scott-Foresman and Company, 1968), pp. 330-36.

[24] E. Laird Landon, Jr., and Robert B. Settle, "Attribution Theory and Consumer Behavior" (Unpublished working paper, University of California, Los Angeles, April 27, 1970).

[25] Published by John Wiley & Sons, Inc., 1958.

constancy of our picture of the world. Attribution theory [26] was elaborated and extended by Harold H. Kelley, who identified four criteria which individuals use to subjectively validate the attributions they make: [27]

1. *Distinctiveness:* The impression of causality is attributed to the thing if it uniquely occurs when the thing is present and does not occur in its absence.
2. *Consistency over time:* Each time the thing is present, the individual's reaction must be the same or nearly so.
3. *Consistency over modality:* His reactions must be consistent even though his mode of interaction with the thing varies. (For example, a detergent is seen to be very effective for washing white and colored clothes, dishes and silverware, walls, floors, automobiles, and paint brushes.)
4. *Consensus:* Attributes of external origin are experienced in the same way by all observers.

The more perfectly the individual's attributions fulfill the criteria, the more confident he will be that he has a valid picture of the world. Settle presents an example to clarify the use of the criteria.[28] If an auto owner observed that his car runs smoothly on Brand A gasoline but knocks and misses with all other brands, he may attribute the causality of smooth operation to Brand A (distinctiveness). Further, if the driver finds that Brand A is associated with smooth operation every time he uses this brand, he will be more confident (consistency over time). If he finds that this effect is present in both city and country driving, this can be seen as consensus over modality. Lastly, he will be still more confident of his attribution if other drivers recognize the same association between the brand and the effect and make similar attributions (consensus). It should be noted that attributions reached through consensus is a two-step process, quite different from the direct experience of the other criteria. Attributions first must be made about the others who are communicating information to him before he can make his attribution. Is the other person consistently honest over time and over many subjects? Can he be trusted? Does he know what he is talking about? Does he have an ulterior motive?

The perception and attribution of causality, the perception of risk, the individual's personality, his experiences, and his expectations, then, are aspects of his cognitive structures which, in turn, constitute one of the more important forces that determine how the consumer will behave in the marketplace.

[26] Much of the material in this section has been adapted or reprinted from Robert B. Settle, "Consumer Attributional Information Dependence" (Unpublished doctoral dissertation, University of California, Los Angeles, 1970) by permission of the author.

[27] Harold H. Kelley, "Attribution Theory in Social Psychology" in *Nebraska Symposium on Motivation, 1967* (Lincoln, Neb.: University of Nebraska Press, 1967), p. 197.

[28] Settle, "Consumer Attributional Information Dependence."

Summary

1. *Perception* is the process by which the individual receives stimuli and gives them meaning based on his previous learning, memories, expectations, fantasies, beliefs, attitudes, and his personality. The determinants of perception are grouped into stimulus factors and functional factors.

2. *Stimulus* factors are derived from the nature of the stimuli, including: (a) *similarity*—we tend to perceive similar things as belonging together, (b) *proximity*—things near each other tend to be perceived as belonging to each other, (c) *continuity*—we tend to perceive stimuli in such a way as to form a whole, and even provide the closure if it is not present, (d) *context*—the setting in which something is found will affect perception, as when we ascribe high or low prestige to advertisements on the basis of the prestige of the magazine in which they appear, and (e) *sensory threshold*—the amount of difference which must exist for us to perceive it varies with the type of product, for example, a $30 difference in the prices of two appliances is much more noticeable than a $30 difference in the prices of two automobiles.

3. *Functional* factors refer to the tendency for the individual to selectively perceive stimuli in such a way as to maintain consistency in his cognitive structure. These factors include: (a) *attention*—we are unable to perceive all possible stimuli, so "filter out" many, (b) *needs*—the level of a need, such as hunger, affects the individual's perception, as when persons deprived of food for long periods perceive more food-related stimuli than others, (c) *preparatory set*—we perceive things as we are "set" to, as when we perceive quality differences which do not exist because we expect differences based on brand names, (d) *perceptual defense*—we tend to perceive stimuli which are consistent with our values, attitudes, and beliefs.

4. An ingenious application of knowledge about perception has been developed in *perceptual mapping*. The methodology provides "maps" of how consumers perceive various brands on two or more dimensions. It is useful for evaluating new product opportunities and for determining the ways consumers perceive this product as similar or dissimilar to another brand, and can provide clues as to how the advertiser might change his brand's image.

5. Consumer behavior is strongly affected by the concept of *perceived risk*. Consumers perceive risk in their buying behavior from (a) their *uncertainty* as to what the buying goals are and their *uncertainty* as to which product or brand will best satisfy the buying goals, and (b) their perception of the *consequences* of a purchase which fails to satisfy the buying goals. Thus perceived risk involves both uncertainty and consequences components.

6. The *attribution* process is one whereby the individual perceives causality in events; for example, a consumer may attribute the smooth operation of his car to a particular brand of gasoline.

5

MOTIVATION
AND
PERSONALITY

Learning and perceiving, as we have seen, influence the final actions of the consumer in his decision to purchase or not to purchase an item, to select one seller over another, or to drink Pepsi Cola rather than Coca Cola. Yet learning and perceiving do not explain adequately why the individual behaves at all. What dynamic driving forces lead one man to go to church on Sundays and another to study catalogs for a power lawn mower to be used on his already well-manicured front lawn? In short, what are his motives?

Motivation may be thought of as the driving force behind behavior, which, in turn, is guided by cognitions and learning as well as group and cultural influences. The individual's consistent reactions to the world about him constitute his *personality*. Unfortunately, because of the interdependencies of the various aspects of consumer behavior, particularly the confounding of motivation and personality, scholars cannot even agree on definitions. The particular philosophy or theory to which a researcher adheres colors his view, his research, his definitions, and his conclusions.

In much of the work done in marketing, and for that matter in psychology and physiology, there has been a tendency to isolate various motives or personality variables (e.g., sexual drive, the need for affiliation, thirst, or prestige) and to study them in their own right or in relation to the pervasive pattern of consumer behavior (such as exposure to media), to the purchase of products (such as mouthwash), or to the choice of particular brands of a product (such as Fords or Chevrolets). However, in actuality a particular personality trait or variable or a particular motive is inextricably related to the total functioning of the consumer, a relationship which must be remembered as one continues with this chapter and this book.

Motivation

Basically, it is to the hypothetical construct of *motive* that we attribute the core of "incitement to action." The purpose of a man's motives—or for that matter his values and attitudes, his needs and emotions, and his behavior in general—is to protect, satisfy, and enhance himself. The key driving force in his behavior is this self-protection and self-enhancement. For example, as a relatively simple process, suppose the sugar content in the individual's blood drops below a specified level. Through a physiological process, he soon begins to perceive that he is "hungry"—a lack, deficiency, or tension exists. Hunger, being an unpleasant state, compels the person to remove the unwanted condition, that is, to eat, or more precisely, to raise the blood sugar level. Motivation is, however, by no means merely a deficiency within the individual's physiological world. To be motivated a person must feel or be "driven" by the necessity to remove the deficiency and achieve equilibrium or *homeostasis*, the tendency of the body to maintain a balance among internal physiological conditions.[1]

A classic example of the physiological pattern of an underlying need leading to a behavior pattern can clearly be seen in the following oft-quoted, albeit tragic, case history.

> A three-year-old boy was brought to the hospital for observation because he showed certain abnormalities. After seven days on a regular hospital diet, the boy suddenly died. Autopsy indicated that the child's adrenal glands were abnormal, causing a loss of salt faster than he could replace it on the hospital diet. The child died of a salt deficiency.
>
> After his death, the parents reported that he had never eaten properly. He hated anything sweet, but rather craved salty things. He eagerly licked the salt off of bacon and crackers, he would eat salt from a salt shaker voraciously and often would scream until someone offered him salt. Meanwhile his parents had discovered that he would eat fairly well only if they put three or four times the normal salt on his food, and in addition, let him eat about a teaspoonful of plain salt a day.[2]

There is little disagreement among psychologists that one large set of motives stems from such biological need systems. These are the physiological drives or tensions that must be reduced if the body is to survive —the relief of excessive heat, cold, and physical harm (pain); the need

[1] Shivering is a good example of a reflexive homeostatic mechanism. If body temperature drops, the individual shivers, hence stepping up his metabolism and the production of heat. It is thought that animals react by fluffing up their fur to create dead air-space. Perhaps goose pimples are remnants of just such a reaction among humans.

[2] L. Wilkins and C. P. Richter, "A Great Craving for Salt by a Child with Cortico-adrenal Insufficiency," *Journal of the American Medical Association*, Vol. 114 (1940), 866-68. As quoted in Clifford T. Morgan, *Introduction to Psychology* (2nd ed.) (New York: McGraw-Hill Book Co., 1956), p. 67.

for air, food, and water; relief of bowel, bladder, and fatigue (sleep), among others.

Several studies have indicated that even in middle class America with its high standard of living there is some relationship between tissue needs and consumer behavior. On the grounds that individuals within a normal weight range tend to eat when they are hungry, Nisbett and Kanouse hypothesized that there would be a positive relationship between hours of food deprivation and the amount of food purchased in a supermarket. They felt that normal individuals are sensitive to internal stimuli which signal hunger and satiety. Under conditions of hunger these shoppers would accumulate or purchase greater amounts of food. In a well-done experiment at a supermarket, the results bore out their hypothesis. Customers who had eaten within an hour of shopping purchased less than $12.00 worth of food as measured on cash register receipts; those with three hours of deprivation purchased about $15.00 worth of goods, and those with more than five hours since eating rang up an average bill of almost $17.00.[3]

Nevertheless, the subject of physiological drives or motives is of little interest to the field of marketing outside of theoretical contributions and perhaps its inherent fascination. Once again, however, we can see the interdependency of the various elements influencing the consumer and guiding his behavior. The interactions of man's social and biological nature can perhaps best be exemplified in his sexual behavior. Basically controlled by a biological hormonal system, his sexual activity is guided by norms, mores, and social customs, as well as learned values and attitudes. The purchase not only of birth control devices, but also of perfumes, deodorants, high-fashion clothing, flashy sports cars, and perhaps even razor blades and toothpaste may be due in part to his sexual drives.

Much as the physiological needs originate in the tissue activity of the human, a second classification or large set of motives, those stemming from the *social* or *psychological needs,* are embodied in the social environment. The demands of the child begin at infancy as his needs for comfort and security emerge. Later he is expected to play with friends, go to school, join clubs, go out on dates, marry, and take his place in society. The immediate gratification of wants, such as a nice home, an expensive car, or an attractive spouse, often must be delayed for much vaguer rewards, such as a college education. In rare cases the motives stemming from psychological or social bases are powerful enough to overcome even the basic physiological drives. Hunger strikes for a social cause or demonstrations in which a person voluntarily exposes himself to police clubs and tear gas are examples of just such behavior.

The complex interlacing of body needs and social and psychological demands on the individual makes any type of classification difficult, and unfortunately researchers and scholars do not agree on classificatory schema. Basically the individual is a total organism, reacting to his

[3] Richard E. Nisbett and David E. Kanouse, "Obesity, Hunger and Supermarket Shopping Behavior," *Proceedings, 76th Annual Convention, American Psychological Association* (1968), pp. 683-84.

internal and external environment. The classification problem involves slicing this dynamic interdependent package of needs, drives, and motives into meaningful subunits. Some scholars, such as Henry A. Murray, have cut the slices rather thin and have, therefore, developed a long series of human needs and motives. Others, such as Sigmund Freud, focus primarily on the biological nature of man, dissecting the motivational structure into much larger slices and, hence, fewer motives.

MASLOW

A widely-quoted view, with which the reader is perhaps familiar, is that of Abraham Maslow.[4] In his theory of human motivation, Maslow felt that man has at least five sets of basic needs; as each level of need is satiated (the physiological needs being the first level), at once other, higher needs emerge. And, in turn, as the new needs are more-or-less satisfied, still newer and higher needs arise. Maslow's central proposition, then, is that basic human needs are arranged in a *hierarchy* of relative prepotency. Hence, if hunger and other biological needs are satisfied, they become unimportant in the dynamics of the individual, and safety needs become predominant, and so on.

The Physiological Needs. Basically this group of needs encompasses the physiological motives or tissue needs discussed earlier in this chapter —food, water, sleep, relief of physical danger, and so forth—most, if not all, of which are homeostatic tension-reducing mechanisms. Maslow felt that the physiological needs are the most prepotent of all needs: a starving man dreams, perceives, and remembers food; problems related to acquiring an automobile, reading textbooks, or buying underarm deodorant seem of secondary importance. Seldom in the United States are these needs truly not satisfied; certainly from a marketing point of view, they tend to be irrelevant.

Safety Needs. If these needs are seriously neglected, the organism can be as wholly dominated by concern over safety needs as it can over physiological needs. This set of needs is based on the seeking of physical safety and security, the seeking of stability in the world, the preference for familiar rather than unfamiliar things or for the known rather than the unknown. Maslow feels that the almost universal tendency to embrace a religion or world philosophy as a coherent, meaningful whole is at least in part motivated by safety-seeking, as is perhaps the purchase of various forms of insurance, securities, and real estate. As these needs

---

[4] Abraham H. Maslow, "A Theory of Human Motivation," *Psychological Review*, Vol. 50 (1943), 370-96; *Motivation and Personality* (New York: Harper & Row, 1954). While we will deal with only one theory, the student should be aware that others are also of value. The work of Henry Murray, for instance, has been the basis for consumer research; see Henry A. Murray, *et al.*, *Explorations in Personality* (New York: Oxford, 1938).

become more-or-less satisfied, the next higher group of needs emerges in this hierarchy.

Love Needs. It is at this stage that a person begins to realize his love, affection, and belongingness needs. He feels keenly the absence of friends, a spouse, children, and a place in the group. Organizations such as the Elks Club, a fraternity, or a gang become most important and perhaps institutions such as marriage and parenthood become prime movers. Although for most individuals in this country the physiological and safety needs are met, for many the love needs are not. And, of course, marketers and advertisers have seized upon this need in the attempt to sell their goods. Seldom does one see ads on how full the advertised product makes one's belly; more often the media are glutted with ads for clothing, soap, perfumes, automobiles, and deodorant, assuring the buyer a place in the group, love, affection, and sexual companionship. Any child weaned on television can assure us that without Ultra-Brite toothpaste, sex appeal is just not conceivable.

Esteem Needs. Once again as the love needs are more or less satiated, the need for esteem, prestige, self-respect, reputation, and status emerge, including the desire for strength, achievement, adequacy, independence, and self-confidence, in addition to recognition and appreciation or esteem in the eyes of others. It relates to the individual's feeling of usefulness in the world. As one achieves love, a sweetheart, and belongingness by the act of purchasing a Mustang, he can now move up to a Cadillac or Lincoln Continental, gaining a feeling of self-confidence, prestige, and esteem in the eyes of others—or so the ads keep telling us.

Self-Actualization. Once all these needs are satisfied, the need for self-actualization will develop: "What a man *can* be, he *must* be." The artist must paint, the teacher must teach, the mother, the carpenter, the scientist must each "do his thing." This need is basically the desire for self-fulfillment, to actualize one's potential, to become everything that one is capable of becoming. To the woman it may be the need to become an ideal mother, to the carpenter perhaps to express himself in his woodwork, to the artist to express himself in his painting or poetry. Of course, according to Maslow, the emergence of this higher-order need depends on the prior satisfaction of all lower-order needs. Few people have reached this pinnacle in their motivational development; hence, it not only carries little relevance to the marketing man, but in fact is rather difficult for those of us who have not reached it to understand. It is at this point that cognitive needs seem to become important—acquiring knowledge, aesthetic satisfaction, learning, philosophizing for the sake of knowledge itself rather than for the sake of prestige or belongingness, and so on.

The Maslow hierarchy, then, reaches from the "belly to the brain." Note that these are *not independent of each other.* As can be seen in Figure 5-1, at any given stage of psychological development other needs are still influential, although only one of the stages is prepotent. For example,

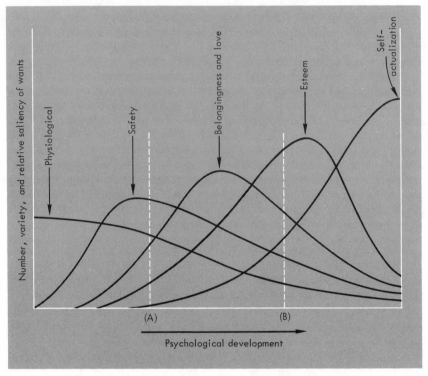

**FIG. 5-1. Schematic Portrayal of the Progressive Changes in Relative
Saliency, Number, and Variety of Wants as Described
by Maslow**

Note: The peak of an earlier main class of wants must be passed before the next
"higher" want can begin to assume a dominant role. As psychological development
takes place the number and variety of wants increase.

Reproduced with permission from David Krech, Richard S. Crutchfield, and Egerton
L. Ballachey, *Individual in Society* (New York: McGraw-Hill Book Company, 1962),
p. 77.

for a person in condition *A*, safety needs are prepotent, but physiological
needs have considerable influence, and the love and esteem needs are
beginning to emerge. As his development reaches condition *B*, the esteem
needs are very potent, self-actualization is beginning to emerge as a need,
but the lower level needs have not completely disappeared as motivating
forces.

Once one begins to consider motivation beyond the molecular level,
it becomes evident that the philosophies or theories held by the scholar
or researcher immediately begin to exert their influence. To discuss
motivation abstractly or independent of theory, then, is not possible,
which immediately necessitates a consideration of the theories of personality since from most points of view these two are inseparable. Maslow

called his classic paper a *Theory of Human Motivation* and yet it is clearly a theory of personality and perhaps even a philosophy of life. In fact, a later work which expounded his views was entitled *Motivation and Personality*. On the other hand, the works of Freud or Karen Horney are often classified as personality conceptualizations and yet primarily involve the motivations behind human behavior.

Personality

Unfortunately, psychologists do not consistently or generally agree on a definition for the concept "personality." [5] However, man's consistency in coping with his environment can be used to establish a workable understanding of the concept: *personality* can, hence, be defined as a consistent pattern of responses to the world that impinges upon the individual from both internal and external sources. It is this consistency of response that allows us to type people as aggressive or submissive, as obnoxious or charismatic. Any given person's reactions to an internal or environmental situation or to a new stimulus depend upon his perceptions of the event. His perceptions, in turn, depend in part upon his usual modes of coping with the environment, since individuals generally react in a consistent or stable fashion in a variety of environmental situations. For example, the cautious, careful, and methodical type of person will usually react cautiously, carefully, and methodically to a new stimulus. Of course, what is of much greater fascination is not the consistency of response, but the very rare occasions in which the individual behaves somewhat inconsistently with his usual stabilized behavior patterns. The professor who, after a few drinks at a party, continues to espouse his stuffy views makes much less a topic of conversation than the reserved professor who unexpectedly begins to chase pretty coeds around the room.

EARLY THEORIES

Personality has fascinated both laymen and scholars for many centuries. The earliest writings of the Chinese, Egyptians, Hebrews, and Greeks related much of behavior to the good and bad spirits that had taken possession of the individual. In fact, an early cure for personality disorders consisted of an operation called *trephining*—the chipping of a round hole in the skull with stones to allow the evil spirits to escape. Other cures included *exorcism,* which involved the ingestion of horrible tasting concoctions, flogging, starving, prayer, and torture to drive the evil spirits out of the body.

[5] Hall and Lindzey, in attempting to deal with the dozens of approaches that exist in the literature, frustratingly submit that *personality is defined by the particular empirical concepts which are a part of the theory of personality employed by the observer.* Calvin S. Hall and Gardner Lindzey, *Theories of Personality* (New York: John Wiley & Sons, 1957), p. 9.

The Greek physician Hippocrates in about 400 B.C. brought forth what is probably one of the first personality theories. He believed that behavior was related to the type of fluid or *humor* (blood, black bile, yellow bile, phlegm) that permeated the body. Although his views were crude and based on inadequate knowledge, they remained popular for some fifteen centuries and perhaps are the precursor of the modern views that much of behavior is related to hormonal balances and blood chemistry.

Other early theories related behavior to body structure or physique (Kretschmer, and more recently Sheldon, were supporters of this opinion) such that short, fat persons tend to be jolly and happy-go-lucky and tall, thin ones are sensitive and shy. Perhaps the most imaginative views came from the phrenologists who claimed that personality is composed of certain faculties or traits, each of which can be found in a specific area of the brain. If a person is pushy or aggressive, the aggressive area of his brain would be enlarged with a concomitant enlargement of the skull at that point. Hence, personality could be measured by proper measurement of the location of bumps on the head.

FREUDIAN THEORY

It was left to Sigmund Freud at the beginning of the twentieth century to develop a view of personality which was to become a major contribution to psychological thought. His writings have not only influenced psychology but have left their impact on literature, social science, and medicine, as well as marketing. Much of the impetus in marketing in the direction of consumer behavior can be traced back to the approaches and methods of the early motivation researchers in the 1940's and 50's. Many of these practitioners and scholars either directly borrowed from Freudian theory and methodology or adopted his philosophies in the modifications of his theory to apply them to marketing; it would be difficult, therefore, to overestimate Freud's historical contributions to consumer behavior.

The psychoanalytic approach of Freud stresses that personality is made up of three main systems of interdependent psychological forces or logical constructs, the *id*, the *ego*, and the *superego*; behavior, then, is a function of the interaction of these three systems.

Id. The id is the original system of the personality and is the source of all its driving psychic energy (the *libido*). Everything psychological that is innate to man, the instinctive cravings, needs, and desires, the brutish impulses that demand immediate gratification—that is, the unrestrained pleasure-seeking impulses—originates in the id. However, man cannot express these basic impulses, his animalistic nature, in society; he would quickly run afoul of its rules, mores, regulations, and values. Hence, a second system of personality is necessary.

Superego. The superego is the internal representative of the traditional values and ideals of society. The function of the superego is to inhibit the impulses of the id that are condemned by those around him.

Actions revolving around sexual and aggressive behavior are a particularly important target of the superego, since the societal mores in these areas are particularly rigid. There is a striving for moralistic perfection as learned from parents, family, friends, teachers, and religious authorities. The superego can be conceptualized as the moral arm of personality, the conscience, the moral sense.

One can perhaps see a conflict within the theoretical and hypothetical structures of the personality: the id, demanding immediate gratification of animalistic drives, versus the superego, attempting to permanently block these pleasure-seeking demands. To the third and final system within the personality is left the resolution of this conflict.

Ego. The ego is a system of forces that functions to control and redirect the id impulses so that gratification can be achieved in the real world, thus resolving the conflict between id and superego. Said to obey the *reality principle,* the ego is the planner, the decider, the thinker, the "executive of the personality because it controls the gateways to action, selects the features of the environment to which it will respond, and decides what instincts will be satisfied and in what manner. In performing these highly important executive functions, the ego has to try to integrate the often conflicting demands of the id, the superego, and the external world." [6] How the ego handles the conflict, how the libidinal energies of the id are guided or displaced accounts for the rich personalities, interests, varied motives, attitudes, and behavior patterns of people.

As consumer products companies became interested in why people buy certain products or prefer one brand over another and in why in the early 1950's brands proliferated and many products became virtually indistinguishable from one another, the psychoanalytic study of basic drives and motivations leading to consumer choice became popular. The Freudian-oriented practitioners stepped in with their tool kits of depth interviews, projective techniques, psychological testing, and advice on packaging, color, distribution, the need for the product, and brand image. Numerous case histories in this body of literature attest to their success, although failures, unfortunately not as prominent in the literature, undoubtedly outnumber the successful advice given to companies. Although today the critics of psychoanalytic applications to marketing far outnumber the adherents and the research methodology of the Freudians in the business world has lessened, marketing still owes a debt to Freud for the advances in marketing theory that his followers and more importantly his critics have contributed.

NEO-FREUDIANS

Within a couple of decades of Freud's early writings, several members of his "inner-ring" of disciples became disillusioned with the master's

---

[6] Hall and Lindzey, *Theories of Personality,* p. 34.

rigid adherence to the biological bases or determinants of personality. Alfred Adler, for example, felt that the basic drive of man is not the channelization of the libido, but rather a striving for superiority. The basic aim of life is, he reasoned, to perfect oneself, that is, to overcome feelings of inferiority imposed during childhood. All other motives and all other drives stem from this striving for superiority. The uniqueness of personality and the variations in behavior stem from the fact that each child is born in a different world and learns different patterns of striving.[7]

Eric Fromm stressed man's loneliness in society. Man's goal is to escape from his bonds of freedom and seek love, brotherliness, and security.[8] This need for interrelationships with other men was most completely developed by Harry Stack Sullivan with his interpersonal theory of psychiatry.[9] The seeking of satisfying human relationships is of central importance to behavior and motivations.

Karen Horney, also one of the social theorists, much like Adler reacted to the biological libido of Freud but, unlike Adler and his emphasis on the striving for superiority, felt that the basic drive of man is coping with anxiety. She felt that the insecurities of childhood stemming from parent-child relations create basic anxieties. An individual's personality develops and lifelong patterns of behavior are formed as he learns to cope with his anxieties and strives to reduce them.[10]

Although the neo-Freudians have had little direct influence on the field of marketing, one does see a number of ads indicating how use of a deodorant soap or a toothpaste reduces feelings of inferiority and creates self-confidence, or how loneliness can be minimized by the use of hair sprays and dyes or Playtex bras.

Horney's views have been best represented in a research project by Joel Cohen, who developed a psychological instrument that purports to measure Horney's three basic orientations towards coping with anxiety. The *compliant* individual desires to be included in the activities of others, to be loved, wanted, appreciated, and needed. The *aggressive* individual copes with anxiety by achieving success, prestige, and admiration; he desires to excel and sees others as competitors. The *detached* person attempts to put emotional distance between himself and others; freedom from obligations, independence, and self-sufficiency are highly valued. Cohen found that compliant people in general prefer brand names and use more mouthwash and toilet soaps. Aggressive types tend to use a manual razor rather than an electric, use more cologne and after-shave lotion, and show preferences for Old Spice deodorant and Van Huesen shirts. The detached types seem to be least aware of brands.

[7] A. L. Ansbacher and Rowens Ansbacher, eds., *The Individual Psychology of Alfred Adler* (New York: Basic Books, 1956).

[8] Eric Fromm, *Escape from Freedom* (New York: Holt, Rinehart and Winston, 1941).

[9] Harry S. Sullivan, *The Interpersonal Theory of Psychiatry* (New York: Norton, 1953).

[10] Karen Horney, *Neurotic Personality in Our Times* (New York: Norton, 1937).

Although his results to date are by no means conclusive, his work does indicate that Horney's theories may have some relevance to marketing.[11]

STIMULUS-RESPONSE APPROACH

The learning-theory, or stimulus-response, approach with a respected history of research and laboratory experimentation supporting it presents perhaps the most elegant view of personality: a conglomerate of responses to specific and generalized cues acquired over time.

According to Dollard and Miller the concepts of cues, drives, responses, and reinforcement are sufficient to explain complex social motives.[12] For example, the need for achievement is learned in the same manner as is brand preference, purchasing habits, or the much simpler types of responses, such as buttoning a jacket or disliking canned peas.

As already mentioned, the first comprehensive models of consumer behavior evolved from a learning-theory approach in the previously discussed Howard-Sheth *Theory of Buyer Behavior,* as well as in the stochastic or probabilistic models and computer simulation techniques.

TRAIT AND FACTOR THEORIES

As the learning-theory approaches have evolved from the tough-minded empirical experimentation of the animal laboratories, so the factor theories have evolved from the quantitative sophistication of statistical techniques and computer technology. The theoretical core is that personality is composed of a set of traits or factors. The theorist begins with a wide array of behavioral measures, typically responses to test items, and by statistical technique distills out traits which are then defined as personality variables. Some of these traits, according to Cattell, are common to all individuals and others are unique to the particular individual.[13] The concept that traits or factors can be quantitatively measured has led to much controversy, in addition to the formation of dozens of personality scales. These tests have been particularly attractive to the more quantitatively-oriented researchers who are attempting to relate personality characteristics to consumer behavior. Although it is difficult to statistically relate the fixation of the libido to brand choice, it is not so difficult to compare consumer behavior patterns to scores on one or another objectively scored personality test. Which technique does a better job is, of

[11] Joel B. Cohen, "An Interpersonal Orientation to the Study of Consumer Behavior," *Journal of Marketing Research,* Vol. 4 (August, 1967), 270-78.

[12] J. Dollard and N. E. Miller, *Personality and Psychotherapy: An Analysis in Terms of Learning, Thinking, and Culture* (New York: McGraw-Hill Book Co., 1950).

[13] Raymond B. Cattell, *Personality: A Systematic, Theoretical, and Factual Study* (New York: McGraw-Hill Book Co., 1950).

course, a moot point and depends on the particular personality theory the researcher holds to be most viable.

Just what degree of influence trait and factor theories have had on consumer behavior emerged best, perhaps, in a study by Evans in 1959.[14] Prior to that time, the work of the motivation researchers seemed to indicate that the underlying personality and motivational structure influenced purchasing behavior in the same manner as it does the selection of a spouse or the use of neurotic defenses. For example, Ford owners were presumed to be impulsive, masculine, and self-confident, while Chevrolet owners were described as conservative, thrifty, prestige-conscious and, along with Plymouth owners, more feminine.

Evans surveyed about 1600 Ford and Chevrolet owners in Illinois, collecting both demographic data and results of the Edwards Personal Preference Schedule. His results indicate that personality needs "are of little value in predicting whether an individual owns a Ford or Chevrolet automobile." Criticism of Evans, however, came from many directions. Martineau, a motivation researcher, had previously concluded that "the buyers and nonbuyers (of automobiles) were undistinguishable except on a personality basis."[15] He criticized the experiment, the study, and the sample. Others criticized Evans' design, his lumping new-car owners and old-car owners together, and his combining models of different years into a single group. Still others objected to his use of a paper-and-pencil personality test rather than a projective instrument.

Westfall, in a sense, replicated Evans' experiment but used another personality instrument, the Thurstone Temperament Schedule rather than the Edwards. Westfall also could not find personality differences between Ford and Chevrolet owners, but did find some important differences between owners of convertible cars on one hand and owners of standard and compact cars on the other: convertible owners tend to be more active, impulsive, vigorous, and sociable than standard car owners.[16]

Tucker and Painter in another study using still another personality measure found a relationship between personality variables and the use of headache remedies, vitamins, mouthwash, alcoholic drinks, chewing gum, and the acceptance of new fashions.[17] Kamen could find no relationship between personality measures on the Thurstone Test and food preferences,[18] while Koponen found significant personality differences between smokers and nonsmokers.[19] Claycamp, in a study of owners of

---

[14] Franklin B. Evans, "Psychological and Objective Factors in the Prediction of Brand Choice: Ford versus Chevrolet," *Journal of Business,* Vol. 32 (October, 1959), 340-69.

[15] Pierre Martineau, *Motivation in Advertising* (New York: McGraw-Hill Book Co., 1957), pp. 66-80.

[16] Ralph Westfall, "Psychological Factors in Predicting Product Choice," *Journal of Marketing,* Vol. 26 (April, 1962), 34-40.

[17] W. T. Tucker and John J. Painter, "Personality and Product Use," *Journal of Applied Psychology,* Vol. 45 (1961), 325-29.

thrift deposits in commercial banks and savings and loan associations, once again found that personality differences do exist among various groups of savers.[20]

In recent research using the personality construct *dogmatism*, developed by Milton Rokeach,[21] Jacoby found that those individuals low in dogmatism were more likely to be innovators in adopting new brands of products.[22] Using the same trait, Bennett has found low-dogmatics more likely to use brands of products and packaging that contribute less to air and water pollution and solid waste problems.

On the other side of the fence, in a massive study by Massy, Frank, and Lodahl on brand preferences of coffee, tea, and beer, the findings were considered disappointing. Just a very small proportion of the variance in purchasing behavior could be accounted for by personality variables.[23]

SELF-CONCEPT

Still other studies have attempted to relate consumer variables to an individual's self-concept; the core of these views is that the individual has a specific perception of himself and his ego. The belief is that individuals perceive products that they own or would like to own in terms of their meaning to themselves and others. If there is a congruence between the symbolic image of the product (e.g., a Corvette is aggressive and masculine; a Lincoln Continental is extravagant and wealthy) and the image he holds of himself, there will be a greater probability for positive evaluations and ownership of that product or brand. Birdwell tested the hypothesis that an automobile owner's perception of his car is essentially congruent with his perception of himself, with the results indicating that here is a high degree of congruence between the two.[24] Grubb found that beer drinkers perceive themselves to be quite different

18 Joseph M. Kamen, "Personality and Food Preference," *Journal of Advertising Research*, Vol. 4 (September, 1964), 29-32.

19 A. Koponen, "Personality Characteristics of Purchasers," *Journal of Advertising Research*, Vol. 1 (1960), 6-12.

20 Henry J. Claycamp, "Characteristics of Owners of Thrift Deposits in Commercial Banks and Savings and Loan Associations," *Journal of Marketing Research*, Vol. 2 (May, 1965), 163-70.

21 Milton Rokeach, *The Open and Closed Mind* (New York: Basic Books, 1960).

22 Jacob Jacoby, "Personality and Innovation Proneness," *Journal of Marketing Research*, Vol. 8 (May, 1971), 244-47.

23 William F. Massy, Ronald E. Frank, and Thomas M. Lodahl, *Purchasing Behavior and Personal Attributes* (Philadelphia: University of Pennsylvania Press, 1968).

24 Al E. Birdwell, "A Study of the Influence of Image Congruence on Consumer Choice," *Journal of Business*, Vol. 41 (January, 1968), 76-88.

from the self-perceptions of their nonbeer-drinking peers.[25] Dolich further tested the congruence relationship between self-images and product brands with the conclusion that there is a greater similarity between self-concept and images of most-preferred brands than images of least-preferred brands.[26]

LIFE STYLE

An integration of the richness of the motivation research type of studies and the tough-minded statistical sophistication of the factor theorists has led to another type of research involving personality, variously called psychographic research or *life style*. Using methods of cluster analysis and factor analysis, the technique consists of dividing the total market into segments based on interests, values, opinions, attitudes, and demographic variables. Pessemier and Tigert [27] and Wells and Tigert [28] have reported some relationships between these life style clusters and market behavior. These studies, and those of others working with these concepts, report that when these attitude-interest personality clusters are correlated with buying behavior, about ten percent of the variance is accounted for.

SOCIAL CHARACTER [29]

In the attempt to relate people types to marketing variables, one other concept, the social character typology of David Riesman,[30] has led to numerous studies in consumer behavior. Although not directly a personality variable but rather a societal variable, many experts in consumer behavior consider social character to be a subset of personality. In brief, the Riesman thesis is that human beings in general can be grouped into three major types of social character, and that each society or culture manifests predominantly one of these types according to its particular phase of development. By *social character* Riesman means the "ways

[25] Edward L. Grubb, "Consumer Perception of 'Self Concept' and its Relationship to Brand Choice of Selected Product Types," in *Marketing and Economic Development: Winter 1965 AMA Proceedings*, ed. Peter D. Bennett (Chicago: American Marketing Association, 1966), pp. 419-24.

[26] Ira J. Dolich, "Congruence Relationships between Self Images and Product Brands," *Journal of Marketing Research*, Vol. 6 (February, 1969), 80-84.

[27] Edgar A. Pessemier and Douglas J. Tigert, "Socio-Economic Status of the Family and Housewife Personality, Life Style and Opinion Factors," *Purdue University Paper Series*, No. 197 (December, 1967), mimeo.

[28] William D. Wells and Douglas J. Tigert, "Activities, Interests and Opinions," *Journal of Advertising Research*, Vol. 11 (August, 1971), 27-35.

[29] Portions of this section have been adapted from Harold H. Kassarjian, "Riesman Revisited," *Journal of Marketing*, Vol. 29 (April, 1965), 54-56.

[30] David Riesman, N. Glazer, and R. Denney, *The Lonely Crowd* (abridged ed.) (New Haven: Yale University Press, 1961). Original published in 1950.

of behavior" or "modes of conformity to the culture and society within which the person exists."

Tradition-direction is prevalent in societies characterized by general slowness of change, dependence on family and kin organization, low social mobility, and a tight web of values. The culture provides ritual, routine, and religion to occupy and orient everyone.

The *inner-directed* society, found in western society emerging from the Renaissance and Reformation until today, is fostered by industrialization, greater social mobility, and less security for the individual. Such a society is characterized by a rapid accumulation of capital (teamed with devastating technological shifts), and by an almost constant expansion: intensive expansion in the production of goods and people and extensive expansion in exploration, colonization, and imperialism. The greater choice this society gives—and the greater initiatives it demands in order to cope with its novel problems—combined with increasing population and increasing opportunity, leads to sharp competition in the job market as well as in private life.

An inner-directed person gains a feeling of control over his own life, and sees himself as an individual with a career to make. However, he goes through life less independent than he seems, for he is obeying and conforming to an internal piloting based on the values and principles he has incorporated. Education, training, child-rearing practices, occupational opportunities, recreation, and economics are so closely correlated in the inner-directed society that the inner-directed person is prepared to live in a rather unstable, unreliable world by finding stability within himself. The inner-directed man does not consume for the sake of consumption but because of status and prestige, as a pathway to success, and has a passionate desire to make things *his*.

The *other-directed person* lives in a different world, one in which there is social mobility, but also a world of servo-mechanisms, electronic computers, and mechanized gadgetry in which production is no longer a problem. It is a world of abundance, in which the individual must learn to live not as a producer but must be carefully taught to live as a consumer. His path to success is not by way of producing a more competitive product but by merchandising a pleasing personality. Getting along with others is the magic key to accomplishment, depending less on what he is and what he does than on what others think of him and how competent he is in the art of being manipulated as well as in the art of manipulating others.

The home is no longer the agent of greatest influence in implanting social values in a child; instead, the peer group has become all-important. The character of the other-directed person is such that the peer groups are looked to for guidance both by the children themselves and by the parents. The group the other-directed person belongs to and whose goals and values he internalizes is made up of his contemporaries. The other-directed person "is kept within his consumption limits not by goal-directed but by other-directed guidance, kept from splurging too much by others' envy and from consuming too little by his own envy of the other." [31]

Kassarjian created advertisements specially designed on a theoretical basis to appeal to inner- and to other-directed persons and found that subjects express a preference for appeals based on their particular social character type. Further, he found very minimal evidence that there seems to be some differential exposure to the various mass media such as radio, magazines, TV, and sections of the newspaper.[32] In a similar study by Woodside there seemed to be no relationship between the use of selected consumer products and social character, although he did find a minimal relationship between advertising appeals and inner- and other-directedness.[33] Donnelly has shown a relationship between a housewife's acceptance of innovations and social character, with the inner-directed person slightly more innovation-prone.[34]

In summary, the relevance of typology to consumer behavior, marketing, or the persuasion process has yet to be demonstrated, although perhaps a case can be made that social character is an important variable.

Summary

1. *Motivation* is the driving force behind behavior. Thus, *motive* is the construct to which we attribute the core of "incitement to action." The major classification of motives is that of the *physiological* and *psychological* (or social).

2. Maslow's theory of motivation postulates a *hierarchy* of needs. In order of the more basic to the higher-level needs, the groups are (a) *physiological needs* (hunger, thirst, etc.), (b) *safety needs* (need for physical safety and security), (c) *love needs* (need for friends, a spouse, children, a place in the group), (d) *esteem needs* (need for strength, adequacy, self-confidence, recognition, and appreciation in the eyes of others), and (e) *self-actualization needs* (the need to express oneself, to "do one's own thing").

3. Other psychologists, such as Murray, have defined personality through the development of more elaborate lists of motives or needs. These theories have led to research methods which have been used extensively in consumer research.

4. A major contributor to personality theory was Sigmund Freud. His theory postulates a personality structure composed of (a) the *id*, the source of all the psychic energy which drives us to action, (b) the *superego*, the internal representation of the traditional values of society, and (c) the *ego*, the controller and director of the id impulses,

---

[31] Riesman, Glazer, and Denney, *The Lonely Crowd*, p. 79.

[32] H. H. Kassarjian, "Social Character and Differential Preference for Mass Communication," *Journal of Marketing Research*, Vol. 2 (May, 1965), 146-53.

[33] Arch G. Woodside, "Social Character, Product Use and Advertising Appeals," *Journal of Advertising Research*, Vol. 8 (December, 1968), 31-35.

[34] James H. Donnelly, Jr., "Social Character and Acceptance of New Products," *Journal of Marketing Research*, Vol. 7 (February, 1970), 111-13.

enabling the individual to achieve gratification in socially acceptable ways. Much of the work of Freud and the neo-Freudians was the basis for the early interest in consumer behavior by the "motivation researchers."

5. Early research on the impact of personality on consumer behavior was devoted to the effect of a host of factors on specific buying practices. The questions of whether or not Ford owners differ from Chevrolet owners, whether convertible and sedan owners differ, whether personality affects the use of headache remedies, vitamins, mouthwash, beer, etc., have all been studied with varying results.

6. *Self-concept* has been applied to consumer behavior, with the principal finding being that individuals tend to express themselves in the products and even the brands that they buy, i.e., "My car is somehow an extension of my personality."

7. David Riesman's *social character* typology has been a fruitful avenue for consumer research. *Inner-directed* persons gain a feeling of control over their own lives and see themselves as individuals; they consume for the sake of status and prestige—as a pathway to success. *Other-directed* persons feel strong needs to get along well with others, and are concerned less with what they are and what they do, but concentrate more on what others think of them. Their consumption is subject to other-directed guidance; they are kept from spending too much by others' envy and from consuming too little by their own envy of others. There is evidence to indicate that inner- and other-directed people show different preferences for advertising media and messages.

6

ATTITUDES
AND
ATTITUDE CHANGE

In this day and age even the most naive person is keenly aware of the importance of values, beliefs, and attitudes on the behavior of man. Too often we have seen conflicts between persons, institutions, and countries directly attributable to conflicting beliefs and attitudes. All of us are aware that a racy sports car has an equivalent dollar cost as a comfortable Chevrolet heavily laden with accessories. To explain why one consumer purchases the sports car and another the Chevrolet involves, among other things, such concepts as attitudes, beliefs, and images, in addition to the cost considerations.

Social psychologists consider attitudes to be among the most basic constructs leading to behavior. In marketing and advertising billions of dollars are spent annually in establishing, reinforcing, and changing the image of products, brands, and manufacturers.

A *belief* (or an opinion) is an emotionally neutral cognition or a "knowledge" that the individual holds about some aspect or object in the environment—that is, the things a person "knows" to be true from his own point of view, consisting of the facts about something as he sees them at a given point in time. Conversely, the sister concept, *attitude*, is by definition not neutral, but rather is insistent, dynamic, and stirred-up. A person may believe that the Black Panthers is a radical revolutionary organization, which, to him, is a fact—a belief—and therefore is neutral in feelings or affect. His attitudes, however, are not neutral; they may be unusually positive or extremely negative. Obviously one can have a belief without an associated attitude about some object, as for example a brand of pencil eraser. The product exists, it may be necessary, but he neither hates it nor loves it. He is not willing to argue or join a conspiracy to destroy the particular brand of eraser and he holds no attitudes towards the object.

It would not be possible, however, to hold an attitude without also holding a belief. Attitudes cannot exist in a vacuum; they must be directed toward something—either as concrete as a brand of automobile or as abstract as the idea of freedom or responsibility. Krech and Crutch-field define attitude as *"an enduring organization of motivational, emotional, perceptual, and cognitive processes with respect to some aspect of the individual's world."*[1] It is a set of regularities of an individual's feelings, thoughts, and predispositions to behave toward some aspect of the world.[2] It is a trigger to action, as toward the purchase of a brand of automobile, a hate of communists that can lead to enlisting in the military, or negative feelings toward the color of one's hair.

With this dynamic, stirred-up characteristic, attitudes immediately define one's position; they are pro or con, for or against, positive or negative—but *not* neutral. Because of their motivational and emotional characteristics, they are not always obvious; that is, the individual may not always be fully conscious of his attitudes. Opinions can be expressed, but attitudes must be inferred from the feeling-tone of verbal expressions or perhaps from the individual's overt behavior.

An attitude is much like a trigger on a rifle: if the conditions are right within the individual's psychological field, if enough pressure is applied, it will lead to action, either overt behavior, or anger, hostility, love, or compassion toward the attitude object. For example, an individual may have mildly negative attitudes towards rice: it is fattening, he does not like its relatively bland taste, and seldom do American cooks prepare it properly. He just does not like rice. His attitudes have a negative *valence.* Perhaps in seeing a motion picture on the cultural habits of Japanese, he may begin to appreciate that rice is a cheap supply of calorie intake, and it can be prepared in numerous forms, perhaps he may even appreciate that no meal is complete without rice. He does not get hostile, worked-up, or emotional, nor does he decide to take violent action against the next Oriental he sees. However, if the psychological field is changed such that his wife serves him pancakes with a side order of mushy rice for breakfast, he may push his plate aside, not eat, and pout. In this instance the conditions are right for his attitude to emerge as an overt behavioral act, although previously his attitudes toward rice were not action-prone.

SALIENCE

Not all attitudes under all conditions hold the same relevance or *salience* for the individual. The negative attitude towards rice is just not relevant while viewing a motion picture on the cultural habits of the Japanese; under these psychological conditions the negative valence of the attitude toward rice has a low degree of salience. When the psychological field is changed such that rice is served for breakfast, his attitude toward rice becomes much more salient, more relevant, and, at least in our example, explodes into a behavioral act.

[1] David Krech and Richard S. Crutchfield, *Theory and Problems of Social Psychology* (New York: McGraw-Hill Book Co., 1948), p. 152.

[2] Paul F. Secord and Carl W. Backman, *Social Psychology* (New York: McGraw-Hill Book Co., 1964), p. 97.

Usually attitudes toward products, and more particularly specific brands, are not salient to the average consumer. He may have slight preferences for one brand of toothpaste over another but typically he either does not hold an attitude or if he does, it is not very relevant or central to his cognitive organization of the world about him. According to Robertson, any existing attitude toward a product or brand is the result of a number of attitudes toward each of the product attributes, such as price, appearance, flavor, and performance. Each of these attributes in turn has varying salience.[3] Thus styling is a highly salient attribute for sports cars, but less salient for washing machines; price may be highly salient for bread but not salt; and fragrance highly salient for perfume but not gasoline. •

Components of Attitudes

Several theorists in the early 1960's presented a slightly different conceptualization of attitudes and beliefs, which has been widely adopted by researchers and writers in the field of consumer behavior.[4] Rather than drawing a sharp demarcation between attitudes and beliefs, these authors felt that it is the attitude itself that consists of various components: a *cognitive* or belief component, an *affective* or feeling component that has an emotional loading, and a *conative* or action-tendency component that refers to the individual's readiness to behave overtly toward the object.

Cognitive Component. The cognitive component of an attitude consists of the package of beliefs the individual holds about the object. Attitudes towards an American automobile include beliefs about horsepower, internal combustion engines, air pollution, suspension systems, collapsible steering columns, freeways, and mountain roads. According to Krech, *et al.*, cognitions about the object of the attitude include *evaluative* beliefs—the attribution of favorableness or unfavorableness, positive or negative valences, "goodness" or "badness": American cars are polluting the atmosphere, causing massive accidents not possible with small cars, destroying trees, and causing the deaths of other living things. Further Krech includes beliefs concerning the appropriate ways of responding to the object: American cars should be outlawed, heavily taxed, physically removed from the highways and byways, and so on.

Affective Component. The feeling component relates to the emotional aspects of the attitude, the emotions that are connected with the object—

---

[3] Thomas S. Robertson, *Consumer Behavior* (Glenview, Ill.: Scott-Foresman and Company, 1970), pp. 63-64.

[4] David Krech, Richard S. Crutchfield, and Egerton L. Ballachey, *Individual in Society* (New York: McGraw-Hill Book Co., 1962); Daniel Katz, "The Functional Approach to the Study of Attitudes," *Public Opinion Quarterly*, Vol. 24 (Summer, 1960), 163-91; Daniel Katz and Ezra Stotland, "A Preliminary Statement to a Theory of Attitude Structure and Change," in *Psychology: A Study of a Science*, Vol. 3, ed. Sigmund Koch (New York: McGraw-Hill Book Co., 1959), pp. 423-75.

good-bad, hate-love, positive-negative, like-dislike—and is the stirred-up physiological side of the individual; the statement "Damned Republican bankers and fascist industrialists are the cause of war, hunger, and strife" reflects this aspect of a political attitude.

Action-Tendency. The action-tendency component consists of the behavioral aspects of an attitude—or more precisely the potential or readiness to respond. If a person holds negative attitudes, he is potentially ready to attack, destroy, or punish the objects and those things associated with it. If his attitudes are positive, he is disposed to help, reward, purchase, recommend to others, and so on. Much of the work in marketing relating purchasing behavior and brand choice behavior has naturally been involved with the action-tendency component.[5]

MULTIPLEXITY

Each of the components of attitudes may vary with respect to their *multiplexity*,[6] that is, the complexity or simplicity of the attitude. Individuals may have a very undifferentiated set of cognitions, feeling-tone, and action-tendency toward some objects, while for other objects the number and variety of elements is most complex. Most Americans have a low saliency and low centrality attitude toward rice, if any attitude exists at all; there is little differentiation between brands and many housewives cannot even perceive a difference between long-grain and short-grain varieties. Such simplistic cognitions might well be unimaginable to a Vietnamese housewife; on the other hand, to her all motor vehicles might be classified as jeeps—good things to have around. The attitude cluster of the American housewife differentiates between brands of cars, models, accessories, and vintage. Attitudes involve not only transportation but status, prestige, horsepower, roadway congestion, neighbors, auto repairmen, and used-car salesmen. The components of the attitudes are multiplex; the clusters of attitudes that are associated with it are complex and include many elements. The cluster may extend to attitudes about "lead-free" gasoline, concerns about smog, and anger toward Detroit auto manufacturers and International Oil Cartels that are responsible for the improper growth of her azaleas. The action-tendency component of these attitude clusters may induce her to vote for sympathetic political candidates, distribute petitions, and pay two cents per gallon more in order to obtain what she believes to be "cleaner gasoline."

---

[5] The reader is referred to two excellent monographs on the relationship of attitudes to brand choice: John G. Myers, *Consumer Image and Attitude* (Berkeley: Institute of Business and Economic Research Special Publications, Graduate School of Business Administration, University of California, 1968); and George S. Day, *Buyer Attitudes and Brand Choice Behavior* (New York: The Free Press, 1970).

[6] Krech, Crutchfield, and Ballachey, *Individual in Society*, p. 142.

The Development of Attitudes

Although perhaps a bit oversimplified, the most cogent and certainly the most beautiful statement on the development of beliefs and attitudes can be found in the lyrics of the song "Carefully Taught" from Rodgers and Hammerstein's *South Pacific*. The adult sings to the child that he must be taught to hate and to fear those people whose eyes are oddly made, or people whose skin is a different shade. It must be drummed in his dear little ear—and from year to year. Most cogently, he must be taught before it's too late, before he is six or seven or eight. The point of the song is that unless the child is carefully taught, he will grow up not knowing that he must hate all the people his relatives hate.[7]

The development and formation of attitudes and beliefs is basically a learning process not at all unlike the learning processes discussed in Chapter 3. However, as Myers and Reynolds emphasize, the overwhelming evidence concerning the acquisition of attitudes supports the contention that learning occurs in a process of the interaction of the individual with others.[8]

FAMILY INFLUENCES

Among all others, perhaps the most influential forces come from the family. For example, in a set of interviews with white grammar school children, Horowitz, in an oft-quoted study, reported the following responses concerning Negroes.[9]

> "Mama tells me not to play with black children, keep away from them."
>
> "Mother doesn't want me to play with colored children. . . . I play with colored children sometimes and Mama whips me."
>
> "Mother and Daddy . . . tell me not to play with colored people or colored person's things."
>
> "Mother told me not to play with them because sometimes they have diseases and germs and you get it from them."

That numerous studies show a high correlation in the attitudes of parents and children surprises no one. Impressively high correlations can be found between parents and children on politico-economic conservatism, religious beliefs, political party orientation, and numerous other topics. A man is born into his political party almost to the same extent

---

[7] Richard Rodgers and Oscar Hammerstein, *South Pacific,* copyright Chappel & Co., Inc., New York.

[8] James H. Myers and William H. Reynolds, *Consumer Behavior and Marketing Management* (Boston: Houghton-Mifflin Co., 1967), p. 148.

[9] E. L. Horowitz, "The Development of Attitudes toward the Negro," *Archives of Psychology* (New York), Vol. 28, No. 194; as cited in Clifford T. Morgan, *Introduction to Psychology* (2nd ed.) (New York: McGraw-Hill Book Co., 1961), p. 533.

that he is born into the membership of his church. Attitudes toward personal hygiene, preferences of food items, attitudes toward boiled vegetables or fried foods, and beliefs about the medicinal value of chicken soup are similarly acquired.

PEER AND GROUP INFLUENCE

Life in a modern society appears to create a proliferation of groups to which the individual belongs or aspires to belong—each with roles, norms, and strong pressures to conform to a given set of behavior patterns and attitudes. Numerous studies both in social psychology and consumer behavior have indicated that the influence of group membership ranges from the acceptance of a belief pattern to the acceptance of a new product or the diffusion of an innovation. Much of this material will be discussed in a later chapter but a well-known example in the marketing literature may be appropriate here. In a massive study of the acceptance of a new drug among physicians, Menzel and Katz found that the diffusion of the drug was most pronounced among doctors with greater numbers of professional contacts with other physicians. The major impact in the adoption process primarily came from the doctor's peers and opinion leaders and only secondarily from journals, advertising, salesmen, etc.[10] It is through the group that many attitudes are learned and reinforced.

Like much of everything else in human behavior, the influence process of groups is multifaceted. Clearly the group has an important influence on the attitudes and values of its members, but on the other hand a person joins the group or forms friendship bonds with those peers or persons who have a value system similar to his own. Very seldom will a young man with strong beliefs about the essential rightness of the Democratic party join the Young Republicans with a somewhat alternative value system no matter how much prettier Republican girls are than Democratic girls. Having hence joined the local Democratic club, new attitudes consistent with his value system are formed and old attitudes are reinforced.

Turning to still larger groupings of people, such as social classes, ethnic groups, and entire cultures, customs, traditions, beliefs, and attitudes are quickly learned; for example, the Catholic and Jew may feel it is not only proper but pleasurable to consume wine while his fundamentalist Protestant counterpart may feel wine consumption is sinful, may feel guilt-ridden, and may find it quite distasteful.

THE INFLUENCE OF PERSONALITY

To claim that "others" mold the attitudes and beliefs of the individual is not to imply that a group or expert authority merely transmits information

[10] S. Stansfeld Sargent and Robert C. Williamson, *Social Psychology* (3rd ed.) (New York: The Ronald Press Company, 1966), p. 256.

to a passive individual in the same manner that instructions are transmitted to a computer through a program. Whether any given attitude is formed or changed depends to some degree upon the personality of the individual. Rokeach has shown that belief systems are determined by a lifetime of experiences. His work was concerned with two types of humans: open-minded and close-minded persons. The close-minded or dogmatic person shows a high magnitude of rejection of opposing beliefs, greater dependence on external authority in his opinions and attitudes, an inability to distinguish the source of a message from the content of the message, and so on. The dogmatic person, the authoritarian, is more rigid, more simplistic, and often more neurotic.[11] That traits such as aggressiveness, introversion-extroversion, submissiveness, and conservatism influence the attitudes a person assumes is obvious enough that they need no elaboration.

The Functional Nature of Attitudes

Attitudes and beliefs along with all other cognitions such as perception, thinking, reasoning, and feeling do not exist in isolation. The entire cognitive organization of the individual with its interacting and interdependent elements serves a function for the individual; if it did not, it would cease to exist.

Without question cognitions and cognitive processes about fluoridation of water supplies, democracy, American business, products, and services serve the function of satisfying needs and wants within the person. To the individual, perhaps even from the moment he is born, the world is not a buzzing, blooming confusion of unrelated stimuli, noises, and inputs. It is estimated that the average person is exposed to more than a thousand advertisements per day; he is told that Crest reduces cavities, but Colgate does it better, that still another brand turns on sex appeal, others brighten teeth, are striped, spotted, and colored. Still others do all and do it better than competing brands. Some are endorsed by dental associations, others by mothers, models, actors, athletes, and children under five years of age. Each in turn advertises that it is the pinnacle of intelligence, rational decision-making, and shrewdness to purchase their brand and forsake others; to buy a competing brand in turn is the ultimate in foolishness and stupidity.

Yet the consumer does not react in horror and confusion. He does not scream in terror at trying to purchase a tube of toothpaste at the drugstore counter. His world is meaningful, organized, and under control. His mechanisms of selective perception, beliefs, opinions, learned responses, attitudes, and personality—in short, his cognitive structures, his cognitive organization—all function in the search for meaning.[12] As pointed out by Barthol and Goldstein in another context, we are staunchly protected by

[11] Milton Rokeach, *The Open and Closed Mind* (New York: Basic Books, Inc., 1960).

[12] F. C. Bartlett, *Remembering* (London: Cambridge University Press, 1932).

our inefficient nervous systems, our prejudices, our lack of attention, and the inalienable right to completely misunderstand, misinterpret, and ignore those aspects of our environment that do not dovetail in with our cognitive organization of the world.[13]

KATZ'S APPROACH

Perhaps the most widely adopted and most cogent presentation of the functions attitudes serve for the individual, his self, and his personality, is presented by Daniel Katz.[14] His attempt is to classify at the level of the underlying psychological motivations the reasons for which people hold attitudes. What needs or tensions do holding the attitudes reduce within the person?

1. *The instrumental, adjustive, or utilitarian function.* This function is a recognition of the fact that people strive to maximize the rewards in their external environment and minimize the penalties. The consumer develops favorable attitudes toward the objects in his world which are associated with the satisfaction of his needs and unfavorable attitudes toward objects which frustrate him or punish him. Brands of products which require constant repairs, have poor quality control, do not function properly, and thwart the owner very soon lead to a negative image or attitude which may in turn generalize to other products by the same manufacturer. Obviously the closer the object is to actual need satisfaction and the more it is clearly perceived as relevant to the satisfaction of needs, the greater are the probabilities of positive or negative attitude formation or change.

2. *The ego-defensive function.* According to Katz, many of our attitudes function to protect our self-image, our ego, from anxieties, unacceptable impulses, and threat. For example, when we cannot admit to ourselves that we have deep feelings of inferiority, we may project those feelings onto some convenient minority group and bolster our own feelings by attitudes of superiority. The formation of this group of attitudes differs essentially from the adjustive attitudes discussed above. The attitudes develop not from experience with the object itself but rather emerge from within the person, and the object toward which the attitude is expressed is merely a convenient outlet for its expression. Certainly much of the advertising for cosmetics and personal hygiene products appear to focus on the ego-defensive functions of attitudes. We are assured confidence, sexual desirability, and safety from offending by the purchase of deodorants, hair spray, mouthwash, pink-colored toilet paper, and other such products.

3. *The value-expressive function.* This function serves to derive satisfaction from expressing attitudes appropriate to the individual's personal

[13] Richard P. Barthol and Michael J. Goldstein, "Psychology and the Invisible Sell," *California Management Review,* Vol. 1, No. 2 (Winter, 1959), 29-35.

[14] Daniel Katz, "The Functional Approach to the Study of Attitudes," *Public Opinion Quarterly,* Vol. 24 (Summer, 1960), 163-91.

value system and to give expression to his concept of himself. The person who considers himself a connoisseur of foods and wines will hold attitudes which are the appropriate indication of his central values. He gains satisfaction from the expression of attitudes which reflect his cherished beliefs and his self-image. He is expressing to others the notion of his self-identity and the kind of person he would like to be or the kind of person he would like other people to think he is. To the young man who lets his hair grow long and "grooves" on teenage jargon and dress, his attitudes may be expressing an assertion of his independence of the "establishment," although to others he may in fact look like a weakling, radical, or blind conformist.

4. *The knowledge function.* Not only do attitudes function in the service of reducing needs and tensions but they also serve to give meaning to what would otherwise be an unorganized, chaotic universe. In this classification, attitudes serve as standards or frames of reference in the search for meaning, the need to understand, the need for clarity, consistency, and a better organization of perceptions and cognitions. Anticommunist attitudes aid us in determining who are the "good guys" and who are the "bad guys" in international conflicts between Arab and Jew, between guerrilla insurgents and a military dictatorship, in conflicts in import regulations, and in giving military aid to questionable governments.

Cognitive Theories of Attitude

For the world to be organized and meaningful for the individual, the various cognitive elements—attitudes, values, perceptions, and propensity toward behavior—must be consistent with each other. Within the past two decades much empirical research and theorizing has gone into the issue of consistency within and between attitude clusters and between attitudes and other cognitive elements and behavior. Ordinarily one does not see members of the Black Panthers in the Ku Klux Klan. Seldom does a racist contribute to the NAACP, unless, of course, he is a politician seeking liberal and Black votes. In the latter case his behavior is not inconsistent. In fact consistency, whether in mathematics, the sciences, or individual cognitions and behavior, is so commonplace that it requires little explanation. One is not surprised that right-wing anti-Semites are also anti-Negro, anti-Mexican-American, anti-liberal Eastern Establishment, anti-labor unions, anti-welfare programs, and that they are pro-fascist foreign governments, in favor of strong-arm police tactics, and perhaps contributors to politically conservative causes—but not the American Civil Liberties Union.

Consistency is so pervasive that when we do discover inconsistencies they appear dramatic and capture our interest, primarily because they stand in sharp contrast to a world of consistency. The light-skinned Black Panther member who joins the white citizens' council we immediately assume to be a spy or an informer; if not, it is inconceivable that he could own allegiance to both. To the nonsmoker, it is inconceivable that a person can believe that smoking leads to health problems and still continue to smoke. Yet to the smoker his behavior is perfectly consistent, for he "knows" that quitting smoking means gaining weight and becoming nervous. Gaining weight leads to heart attacks, and nervousness leads to a psychosis and a divorce. In turn, a psychosis or a heart attack is far more serious a risk than a "one-in-a-million chance" of lung cancer. Hence, it is perfectly consistent to continue to smoke, in fact it is for his health and welfare that he continues to buy cigarettes.[15] As inconsistent as his actions may seem to others, to the individual his cognitions, his attitudes, and the components of his attitudes may be internally consistent and consistent with his behavior.

The first researcher to discuss consistency (balance, congruity, or cognitive dissonance as it is alternatively termed) was Fritz Heider.[16] Heider's balance model is such that one person perceives two others with some sort of relationship among the three. If he likes both, he expects them to like each other. *A balanced state* is one in which the perceived relationships are internally consistent. An *imbalanced state* occurs if person A likes persons B and C, but B and C dislike each other. This would be an unstable cluster leading to motivations in the direction of cognitive balancing; B and C have got to like each other or A must move toward disliking either B or C.

From this theoretical structure, one could readily assume that in the purchase of a new product or a complex product (such as a TV set, air conditioning equipment, or complicated gadgetry) positive comments from a respected source could lead to positive attitudes about the product, and there would be greater propensity to purchase that product over one about which the source had many negative comments. Perhaps this is obvious, for we all might agree that if a respected expert claimed that one brand of an unknown but needed product was superior to another and other variables such as price and availability were equal we would lean toward the purchase of that brand. In fact, there is considerable research in the marketing literature supporting this view.

Other researchers extended Heider's work.[17] For example, Rosenberg's view of consistency concerns itself with what happens when attitudes change. He extended the cognitive component of an attitude to include not only cognitions about the object of the attitude but also beliefs about the relations between the object and other important values of the person.

---

[15] This example is not as farfetched as it may first appear. Quite similar results can be found in Harold H. Kassarjian and Joel B. Cohen, "Cognitive Dissonance and Consumer Behavior: Reactions to the Surgeon General's Report on Smoking and Health," *California Management Review,* Vol. 8 (Fall, 1965), 55-64.

[16] Fritz Heider, "Attitudes and Cognitive Organization," *Journal of Psychology,* Vol. 21 (1946), 107-12.

[17] D. Cartwright and F. Harary, "Structural Balance: A Generalization of Heider's Theory," *Psychological Review,* Vol. 63 (1956), 277-93; Theodore M. Newcomb, "An Approach to the Study of Communicative Acts," *Psychological Review,* Vol. 60 (1953) 393-404; Charles E. Osgood and Percy H. Tannenbaum, "The Principle of Congruity in the Prediction of Attitude Change," *Psychological Review,* Vol. 62 (1955), 42-55; Herbert C. Kelman, "Processes of Opinion Change," *Public Opinion Quarterly,* Vol. 25 (Spring, 1961), 57-78.

The implication is that there is a consistency between the beliefs, attitudes, and values held by the person as well as a consistency within the components of the attitude. If instability or inconsistency does exist, it will lead to a change in one of the elements or components, such as attitude change itself, rejection of persuasive communications that may have caused the instability, or some other cognitive change that will lead to stability.[18] In Rosenberg's view attitude change comes about in the effort to seek consistency. For example, suppose a person has an intense dislike for foreign-made products, particularly for items made in Japan. Further, suppose he reads in a highly-respected electronics magazine that Panasonic stereo tuners are rated to be of the highest quality. Under these conditions some form of attitude change is likely. Either his positive attitudes toward the magazine, or his negative attitudes toward the particular Japanese product, or perhaps even his generalized attitude toward "Made in Japan," are likely to be shaken.

Fishbein, a social psychologist at the University of Illinois, has developed an attitude model quite similar to that of Rosenberg. According to Fishbein, an attitude consists of two components, *beliefs* about the attributes of the object and an *evaluation* of the beliefs.[19] Hence, a consumer's attitude toward, say, a brand of stereo equipment is a function of his beliefs about the product in terms of the attributes the product possesses and the importance of these attributes. If other conditions, such as having enough money and a need to buy the item, are present, he will move toward (purchase, try out, recommend) the brand for which he has the most favorable attitude and away from (not purchase or recommend) those for which he has less favorable attitudes.

The model can be represented algebraically:

$$A_0 = \sum_{i=1}^{n} B_i \cdot a_i$$

where

A_0 = the attitude toward some object o (a brand, item, or product).

B_i = belief i about o, that is the probability that the object o is related to some other object (the belief that the brand has some attribute).

a_i = the evaluative aspect of B_i, the evaluation of a specific belief (that the brand possesses this attribute is good).

n = the number of attributes (beliefs) important in the selection of the product.

[18] Milton J. Rosenberg, "A Structural Theory of Attitude Dynamics," *Public Opinion Quarterly*, Vol. 24 (Summer, 1960), 319-40; Milton J. Rosenberg and R. P. Abelson, "An Analysis of Cognitive Balancing" in *Attitude Organization and Change*, eds. Carl I. Hovland and Irving L. Janis (New Haven: Yale University Press, 1960), pp. 112-63.

[19] Martin Fishbein, "Attitude and the Prediction of Behavior," in *Readings in Attitude Theory and Measurement*, ed. Martin Fishbein (New York: John Wiley and Sons, 1967), pp. 477-92.

The various attributes a product possesses can be investigated sumed (for example, toothpaste attributes are decay prevention color, flavor, price, teeth-whitening ability, among others). And consumers can be asked how important, satisfactory, or unfavorable each of these attributes are for a given brand, a great deal of research has emerged in the marketing literature in the past two or three years using Fishbein's approach.[20] It appears that individual brand preference can be predicted with a high degree of reliability.

COGNITIVE DISSONANCE

Among the balance theories, Festinger's theory of *cognitive dissonance* has led to the greatest amount of subsequent experimentation in social psychology and to numerous research studies and papers in the field of consumer behavior.[21] Although very similar to the other theories, dissonance is applied only to post-decision inconsistency. All of us have learned to admire the newly purchased car of a friend. He demands from us reassurance that he has made a wise decision, that the car is excellent for the price he paid, and that he is a shrewd buyer. It would be the ultimate folly to imply that he was a fool for making the ridiculous purchase he did. According to Festinger, all the positive attributes of the cars he considered but did not purchase and all the negative aspects of his purchased vehicle are dissonant with his purchasing behavior. In his seeking reassurance from friends that his purchase was a wise one, he is attempting to reduce the post-purchase cognitive dissonance.

Assuming that a purchaser of an automobile experiences dissonance and looks for reassurance, it is natural to expect him to be highly receptive to advertising provided by the manufacturer. In the ad for the car he has just purchased, the superiority of the product and the wiseness of his decision would be bolstered. A study by Ehrlich, et al.,[22] found just these results: purchasers of new cars read and noticed more ads for

[20] Joel B. Cohen and Olli T. Ahtola, "An Expectancy X Value Analysis of the Relationship between Consumer Attitudes and Behavior," in *Proceedings, Second Annual Conference*, ed. David Gardner (Association for Consumer Research, 1971), pp. 344-64; Reza Moinpour and Douglas L. Machlachlan, "The Relations among Attribute and Importance Components of Rosenberg-Fishbein Type of Attitude Model: An Empirical Investigation," in *Proceedings, Second Annual Conference*, ed. David M. Gardner (Association for Consumer Research, 1971), pp. 365-75; Frank M. Bass and W. Wayne Talarzyk, "Using Attitude to Predict Individual Brand Preference," *Occasional Papers in Advertising*, No. 4 (May, 1971), 63-72; and Jerome E. Scott and Peter D. Bennett, "Cognitive Models of Attitude Structure: Value Importance *is* Important," in *Combined Proceedings: 1971 Spring and Fall Conferences*, ed. Fred C. Allvine (Chicago: American Marketing Association, 1972), pp. 346-50.

[21] Leon Festinger, *A Theory of Cognitive Dissonance* (New York: Harper and Row, Publishers, Inc., 1957).

[22] D. Ehrlich, I. Guttman, P. Schonbach, and J. Mills, "Post-Decision Exposure to Relevant Information," *Journal of Abnormal and Social Psychology*, Vol. 54 (1957), 98-102.

the brand of car they had just purchased than for competing brands which they had considered but did not purchase.[23]

Festinger proposes that the existence of dissonance, being psychologically uncomfortable, will motivate the person to try to reduce the dissonance and achieve consonance through a number of methods. First, an individual can reduce dissonance by eliminating or reevaluating one of the cognitive elements or his responsibility or control over the act or decision, a method which has been studied in connection with electrical appliances.[24] Second, information can be denied, distorted, or forgotten in the service of dissonance reduction. Kassarjian and Cohen found this with smokers' denial of the link between smoking and lung cancer.[25] As a third method, dissonance can effectively be reduced by minimizing the importance of the issue or decision that led to the dissonant state. Finally, new cognitive elements can be added to support the decision; once a new car is purchased, the buyer begins to read technical information, brochures, and ads to buttress his decision.

In summary, attitudes, beliefs, and cognitions tend to be consistent with each other and with behavior. Inconsistencies which do exist are uncomfortable states which the individual attempts to change either by adding new cognitions, changing his behavior, distorting dissonant information, or by changing his attitudes and beliefs.

Attitude Change

The topic of attitude change has been of serious concern to both scholars and practitioners for many years. Organizations such as the Anti-Defamation League, the NAACP, and the National Conference of Christians and Jews serve at least a partial function of attitude change. Professional propagandists, public relations men, political campaign managers, and advertising agencies exist primarily for the purpose of attitude change. If one considers the dollars spent for advertising worldwide, by governmental agencies such as the United States Information Agency, the Ministries of Information and Propaganda of just a few major countries, and the campaign budgets of politicians, the total amount undoubtedly must be measured in hundreds of billions. Add to that the average individual's concern with changing the attitudes of friends or spouse, and it is no wonder that attitude change is a topic of major concern to the individual, to politicians, and to marketers.

Some aspects leading to attitude change have been hinted at in the previous section. Any thorough examination would require a book many

[23] Engel could not find other measures of dissonance among new car purchasers but his results did show that new car owners showed higher recall of dealer advertisements. James F. Engel, "Are Automobile Purchasers Dissonant Consumers?" *Journal of Marketing*, Vol. 27 (April, 1963), 55-58; James F. Engel, "Further Pursuit of the Dissonant Consumer: A Comment," *Journal of Marketing*, Vol. 20 (April, 1965), 33-34.

[24] J. W. Brehm, "Post-Decision Changes in the Desirability of Alternatives," *Journal of Abnormal and Social Psychology*, Vol. 52 (July, 1956), 384-89.

[25] Kassarjian and Cohen, *California Management Review*, Vol. 8, 55-64.

times the size of this one. Yet perhaps we should summarize some of the things we know or think we know about the topic. Attitude change will be discussed from the approach of the change agent, aspects of communications content, and from the approach of the interpreter or recipient of the influence.

THE CHANGE AGENT

Among the most powerful of the change agents influencing attitudes are the groups to which an individual belongs or aspires to belong. The high school girl, at one point in time horrified at the thought of wearing pants or skirts above the knee, may very rapidly change her attitude system to an insistence on wearing skirts just several inches below the waist, and then just as rapidly insist that skirts be no more than a few inches above her ankles, in conforming with the prevalent style worn by her contemporaries. The influence of others on conformity to group values and attitudes has been heavily researched and often utilized effectively by advertisers. One need not watch television long to realize that not using Ban deodorant, Colgate toothpaste, or sundry brands of hair spray and hair oils will not only lead to sexual deprivation but also to complete rejection by the group.

One of the concepts behind enforced integration of public schools in this country has been the expectation that wider knowledge, interaction, and shared experiences will lead to a lessening of hostile attitudes and stereotypes, and to an increase in understanding and acceptance among races. Similar expectations have come to pass in the Armed Forces, housing projects, religion, and education. Newcomb in a classic study at Bennington College has demonstrated that freshmen from largely urban upper-income families shifted their social attitudes to liberal views on social and political issues by the time they became seniors, concurrent with the views of advanced students and professors.[26] Siegel and Siegel have demonstrated in a study at Stanford University among dormitory groups and "row houses" that the attitudes of the girls were determined both by the groups they belonged to and the groups they wanted to belong to.[27]

Turning from the face-to-face influence of the group to mass communications, one can only be impressed by the influence the mass media have had on the consumer through whatever mediating influences they may operate. The communicator as a change agent has been heavily researched. The voice, the mannerism, accent, reputation, occupation of the communicator, the media used, and the mode of presentation all seem to be relevant to behavior and attitude change. What is more fascinating,

---

[26] Theodore M. Newcomb, *Personality and Social Change: Attitude Formation in a Student Community* (New York: Dryden, 1943).

[27] Alberta E. Siegel and Sidney Siegel, "Reference Groups, Membership Groups and Attitude Change," *Journal of Abnormal and Social Psychology*, Vol. 55 (1957), 360-64.

however, is not that certain characteristics of the communicator make a difference in our susceptibility to persuasion but rather that often extremely negative characteristics can have a positive influence. How many times have we all seen obnoxious, incredible ads and swore never to buy a used car from that particular dealer or never under any circumstances ever to buy, say, Dristan or Anacin? And yet, we do buy used cars, Anacin, Dristan, detergents, and deodorants at a rate that continually encourages nauseous advertising. The source may have zero credibility and yet perhaps may be able to influence our purchasing behavior in spite of felt attitudes.

Hovland and Weiss in an old but classic study examined the influence of source credibility in a rather systematic manner. They presented two alternative versions of communications on the topics of antihistamine drugs, atomic submarines, steel, and the future of movie theaters, one presenting an affirmative position and the other a negative position. The highly credible sources of information used were a medical journal, a renowned scientist, the Bulletin of the National Resources Planning Board, and *Fortune* magazine; the low-credibility sources were a pictorial magazine, *Pravda*, a right-wing newspaper columnist, and a gossip columnist. Immediately after the exposure larger changes of opinion for the high-credibility than for the low-credibility sources were found; twenty-three percent of the participants changed their opinion in the direction of the highly credible source. However, four weeks later the experimenters discovered a decrease in the amount of agreement with the trustworthy source and an increase in the amount of agreement with the untrustworthy source. After the time interval, no differences existed in the amount of opinion change achieved by the two sources. Apparently with the passage of time the influence of the communications source becomes less important than the content.[28] The experiment has been replicated several times on various topics with strikingly similar results and the process has been dubbed the "sleeper effect." Perhaps some forms of advertising appear to be effective in spite of the communicator rather than because of him.

COMMUNICATIONS CONTENT

Considerable research in attitude change as well as advertising and propaganda has been related to the content of the communications material itself. How should a message be worded? Should competitive brands be mentioned by name? Can scare techniques be effective or will they boomerang? Entire research techniques, such as content analysis and copy testing, have been developed relative to the issue of communications content.

[28] Carl I. Hovland and Walter Weiss, "The Influence of Source Credibility on Communication Effectiveness," *Public Opinion Quarterly*, Vol. 15 (Winter, 1951-1952), 635-50.

One-sided versus two-sided communications. Very seldom in advertising does one find a two-sided communication; the weaknesses of the advertised brand and the strengths of the competing brands are rather neatly avoided. However, this may not be the best strategy under all conditions. Several studies have indicated that in general whether one-sided or two-sided presentations are made, the amount of attitude change achieved is about the same. However, among those subjects who were originally in favor of the advocated position, one-sided communication tended to be most effective, but among those who were originally hostile to the position, two-sided communication was more effective. In addition, the more educated subjects tended to be more influenced by two-sided communications and the less educated more convinced by one-sided material.

Turning to inoculation against persuasion from a competitor, the studies seem to indicate that two-sided communications were far more effective in protecting the individual from counterpropaganda or counter-communications. In other words, when subjects were originally presented with both sides of an issue, their change in attitude in the direction of the communicator's intent was not affected by the "competitor's" message. On the other hand, when only one side was presented the countercommunication completely wiped out the original effect of attitude change.

In the attempt to relate this material on attitude change to the world of advertising and marketing, Bither, Dolich, and Nell recently conducted a well-designed experiment involving both the reinforcement and the attack of strongly held attitudes toward the censorship of motion pictures. They concluded that, contrary to widely held beliefs in advertising, two-sided communications are indeed more effective than one-sided communications, and that, when advertising is designed as an immunizing agent, the marketer need not fear that the two-sided message will cause a decrease in belief level. In addition, the authors state that a two-sided appeal is more effective in maintaining the belief level when a counterattack is likely to follow, such as in the case of a competitive industry which makes heavy use of the mass media.[29]

Order of presentation. When a competitor's message is being presented along with our own, are we better off when our communication is presented first or last? Hovland wrote an entire volume on this problem [30] and numerous studies have appeared since. Both have advantages: one often remembers best the last thing he is told, but on the other hand one may walk away or not listen very closely after the first appeal. Research in advertising has indicated that the superior ad is most influential, no matter what its location in a series, but where the ads are equal in

---

[29] Stewart W. Bither, Ira J. Dolich, and Elaine B. Nell, "The Application of Attitude Immunization Techniques in Marketing," *Journal of Marketing Research,* Vol. 8 (February, 1971), 56-61.

[30] Carl I. Hovland, ed., *The Order of Presentation in Persuasion* (New Haven, Conn.: Yale University Press, 1957).

quality, the results are equivocal. In general no simple conclusion can be drawn from this body of data, but further research is underway.

Amount of change advocated. On topics and attitudes which are not deeply seated or central to the individual, Hovland and Pritzker found that the greater the change advocated, the greater the change produced.[31] On unimportant issues—and much of marketing may consist only of issues unimportant to the consumer—if the advertiser advocated a large change in attitudes and opinions, he will be more successful than if he advocates a rather small change from the present position of the individual. However, these results are not confirmed in studies where the attitudes being manipulated are those in which the individual is deeply involved, and in fact, if the attitudes are truly important to the individual, advocacy of an extreme change may lead to a *boomerang* effect: on relevant issues where there is a very marked discrepancy between the position of the communicator and that of the individual, attitude change may occur in the opposite direction from that advocated by the propagandist. For example, "Surrender" leaflets dropped during World War II to demoralize the population typically had the effect of boosting the morale of the recipient and increasing his will to resist.

The effects of fear. Personal hygiene products, such as deodorants, beauty soaps, sanitary napkins, and hair dressings, often use fear as their primary appeal. Not using a particular brand will lead to most dreadful consequences related to health, social status, and social appeal. Yet, the evidence on the effectiveness of using a scare or fear appeal is not unequivocal.[32] In a now-classic study, Janis and Feshbach presented the consequences of improper dental hygiene by using mild, moderate, and strong fear appeals. Results indicated that the stronger the fear induced, the less the subjects adhered to the recommendations in the film.[33] On the other hand Stuteville reports that the fear of spoiled canned tuna in the 1960's and the cancer–cranberry scare in the late 1950's almost destroyed the tuna and cranberry industries.[34]

INTERPRETER CHARACTERISTICS

The content of the message, the signs and symbols, cannot be viewed in isolation. The results of the studies on communications clearly indicate that there is an interaction or confounding between the message content

[31] Carl I. Hovland and H. A. Pritzker, "Extent of Opinion Change as a Function of Amount of Change Advocated," *Journal of Abnormal and Social Psychology*, Vol. 54 (1957), 257-61.

[32] Michael L. Ray and William L. Wilkie, "Fear: The Potential of an Appeal Neglected by Marketing," *Journal of Marketing*, Vol. 34 (January, 1970), 54-62.

[33] Irving L. Janis and Seymour Feshbach, "Effects of Fear Arousing Communications," *Journal of Abnormal and Social Psychology*, Vol. 48 (January, 1953), 78-92.

[34] John R. Stuteville, "Psychic Defenses against High Fear Appeals: A Key Marketing Variable," *Journal of Marketing*, Vol. 34 (April, 1970), 39-45.

and the characteristics of the interpreter or audience. This is perhaps most evident in the material on fear appeals just discussed. Persuasibility seems to be related to low self-esteem, hostility and aggressiveness, perceptual dependence upon others, submissiveness, social isolation, lower intelligence levels, and with women rather than men.[35] Basically the issue appears to be related to the functions the attitudes have for the individual. Those attitudes that are important in his search for meaning would be difficult to change. If the attitudes are positively related to cognitive consistency or balance, change is difficult. On the other hand, attitudes that lead to cognitive imbalance or dissonance may well be easier to manipulate. If one is considering Katz's classification of ego-defensive attitudes—those that protect the individual against internal conflicts and dangers—and value expressive attitudes—those that help maintain his self-identity—the changing of attitudes may well require a basic personality change within the individual. This is most difficult to bring about, especially with the methods available to the marketer.

Attitude Change and Behavior Change

Social scientists and marketing scholars and practitioners have long assumed that there is necessarily a relationship between attitude change and behavior change. Experimental evidence has indicated, interestingly, that behavior change will often lead to attitude change. But the reverse, whether attitude change leads to behavior change, has not been unequivocally demonstrated. Because an advertiser is able to inculcate positive attitudes and a positive image within a consumer does not necessarily mean that the consumer will actually buy his product. There is data to show that he may be more predisposed to purchase, he may claim intentions to purchase, but whether the actual behavioral act of purchase occurs is not known. The problem seems to be that there is insufficient research to make a definitive statement. For example, we would accept that any of several attitudes, needs, or environmental circumstances could lead to the same behavior, say, the selection of an airline. On the other hand, *a specific attitude could lead to several behavior patterns.* Dislike of a particular airline could lead to selection of several competitive airlines, to travel by car, bus, train, or even to beer consumption, as the consumer reacts by not traveling at all but rather by watching television and drinking beer. Much of the research to date has attempted to take a single attitude cluster and correlate it with a single behavior pattern with poor correlations and negative results. Certainly no one denies the importance of attitudes and attitude change for business as well as other institutions and most certainly it is a most important aspect of consumer behavior as a field of inquiry.

[35] Carl I. Hovland, Irving L. Janis, and Harold H. Kelley, *Communication and Persuasion* (New Haven, Conn.: Yale University Press, 1953) as summarized by S. Stansfeld Sargent and Robert C. Williamson, *Social Psychology* (3rd ed.) (New York: The Ronald Press Company, 1966), pp. 284-86.

Summary

1. *Attitude* has been defined as "an enduring organization of motivational, emotional, perceptual, and cognitive processes with respect to some aspect of the individual's world."

2. Attitudes have a *cognitive* or "knowledge" component, an *affective* or "feeling" component, and a *conative*, or "action-tendency" component.

3. Attitudes are *learned*, primarily through interaction with others, particularly family and peer groups.

4. The major *functions* which attitudes serve for the individual are: (a) the *instrumental function*, helping to satisfy needs; (b) the *ego-defensive function*, helping to protect the self-image; (c) the *value-expressive function*, giving expression to self-concepts; and (d) the *knowledge function*, giving meaning to what would otherwise be an unorganized, chaotic world.

5. *Cognitive balance*, or consistency, is essential to the individual's psychological comfort. His attitude structure must be consistent, and he will, therefore, strive to bring balance to any inconsistent state.

6. Social psychologists, principally Rosenberg and Fishbein, have developed theories of attitude structure which state that attitudes are a function of *beliefs* (cognitions) about the attitude object and *evaluative aspects* (affect) of those beliefs. In *marketing*, a consumer's attitude toward a brand is a function of his beliefs about the brand's possession of certain *attributes*, and the *importance* of those attributes.

7. Festinger's theory of *cognitive dissonance* has been applied to marketing. After a choice has been made, a consumer will suffer *post-decision* dissonance from favorable information about the brands *not* purchased and from unfavorable information about the brand actually purchased. He will be motivated to eliminate this dissonance through one or more psychological mechanisms.

8. *Attitude change* is the central purpose of much marketing activity. Extensive research has emphasized the roles played in the process of attitude change by (a) the *change agent*, or source of the message; (b) the *content* of the message; and (c) the *interpreter*, or audience.

9. The attitude *change agent* is most often a respected or important source, such as a peer group or a respected authority. The *amount* of attitude change is related to the credibility of the source of the message; however, it has been found that after passage of time these source effects lose their importance.

10. The *content* of communications, including advertising and selling, has been the subject of much research. Some useful concerns are the impact of (a) one-sided versus two-sided communications, (b) the order of presentation when opposing arguments are to be heard, (c) the amount of change advocated in the message, and (d) the use of fear as an appeal.

11. The *interpreter* of communications must also be considered. The

audience's perceptions of messages and the differences in *persuasibility* among its members affect the results of the communication.

12. The major purpose of changing attitudes is to eventually change *behavior*. This link is difficult to establish, however, especially when situational factors impede behavior which might have resulted from a change in attitude.

7

GROUP INFLUENCES

Up to this point the individual factors that influence the consumer have been emphasized. However, the individual does not function as an entity independent of those around him; his contact with others, ranging from members of his family or living group to fellow workers, neighbors, and sales clerks to complete strangers, is constant. A casual comment such as, "What an attractive blouse," or "That's a becoming jacket," from a bus driver, friend, or family member may very well influence his next purchase far more than his share of thousands of dollars of an advertising budget. The purpose of this chapter is to examine influence of others on the individual—both the influence of the group on the individual consumer and the personal influence exerted by one person upon another.

AGGREGATES, GROUPS, AND SOCIAL ORGANIZATIONS

A haphazard collection of people is *not* a group. Although the other fans at a hockey game or a boxing match may influence what a given fan wears that evening or what he purchases at a refreshment stand, the audience must be characterized not as a group but rather as an *aggregate collection*. Social psychologists reserve the term *group* for "two or more people who bear an *explicit psychological relationship to each other*." [1] For example, a student in Pennsylvania may have no psychological existence for another student in California. They do not know each other, are unaware of each other's being, and cannot directly influence each other. Although both are students, they are not members of a group. It may occur, however, that these two individuals quite independently decide to attend a peace rally to be held in a third state, where they both get arrested and share a cell along with still others. It is quite possible that

[1] David Krech and Richard S. Crutchfield, *Theory and Problems of Social Psychology* (New York: McGraw-Hill Book Co., 1948), p. 368.

a group may emerge from this collection and from the group a leader. They have become aware of each other, of each other's needs, values, and norms; common needs and goals may emerge, each person beginning to dynamically interrelate with the others—to perceive the others as members of the group. Thus, the definition of a group is (1) persons who are interdependent upon each other such that each member's behavior potentially influences the behavior of each of the others, and (2) the sharing of an ideology—a set of beliefs, values, and norms—which regulates their mutual conduct.[2]

As the members of the group interact toward accomplishing a common objective or task, an ideology usually develops which may become to a greater or lesser degree unique to that group alone, setting it apart from other groups. Religious groups, sororities, friendship circles, poker clubs, neighbors, cliques within larger organizations, educational, recreational, and political collections of people may meet these criteria and be defined as groups.

A still larger collection of people, often consisting of many groups, can be defined as a *social organization*, an example of which is a manufacturing plant, consisting of many groups such as friendship circles, labor unions, executive clubs, secretaries' associations, and perhaps others not affiliated with any specific group. The organization is typically characterized by the possession of (1) cultural products (such as buildings, robes, prayers, magic formulas, songs), (2) a collective name or symbol, (3) distinctive action patterns, (4) a common belief system, and (5) enforcing agents or techniques.[3]

STRUCTURE AND FUNCTION

For any group to survive it must serve important, and sometimes vital, functions for the individual. Of course, some groups may be involuntary, such as a family, prison, or military unit, but even involuntary groups serve some needs of the individual. A family unit provides biological maintenance, a means of socialization, security, and a feeling of belongingness, among others. The function of a sorority is primarily social, but obviously it serves other needs as well: it may have important educational functions, contacts for future employment, membership for proper social circles, biological maintenance, and even information on the purchase of a new automobile. "Often the secondary or accessory functions of a group are more important than its formal objectives. The problems caused by swelling enrollment in our colleges and universities might vanish overnight if the rewards of college attendance were limited to the joys of intellectual discovery, and did not include refuge from military service, sexual opportunity, social status, job advancement, and so on." [4]

[2] David Krech, Richard S. Crutchfield, and Egerton L. Ballachey, *Individual in Society* (New York: McGraw-Hill Book Co., 1962), p. 383.
[3] Krech and Crutchfield, *Theory and Problems of Social Psychology*, p. 369.
[4] Harold H. Kassarjian and Thomas S. Robertson, *Perspectives in Consumer Behavior* (Glenview, Ill.: Scott-Foresman and Company, 1968), p. 273.

Obviously a group may fulfill different needs for various individuals; however, in most cases no one group can fulfill all the needs of each of the members, hence most of us belong to many groups. One individual, a member of both of the Young Democratic and Young Republican Clubs on a college campus, claims that his political values are most closely met by the Democratic Club, but the Republicans have much prettier (and richer) girls.

Each group exerts on the individual a variety of influences, pressures to conform, and forces that help guide his behavior, whether it be voting, rioting, cutting his hair, purchasing a deodorant, or selecting a spouse.

Conformity to the Group

For a group to continue in existence it must exert pressure on the individual to conform to its ideology. In a voluntary group, if the individual does not agree with the belief and value systems of the group, he is free to leave and is in fact encouraged to do so by the other members. Coercion is seldom necessary, of course, since the individual joined the group because he perceived the group as having a need-fulfilling function similar to his own beliefs and ideology in the first place. Nevertheless, each group does have enforcing agents, techniques, and sanctions for improper behavior. For the social group it may be ridicule, snickering, gossip, and perhaps even a formal vote for expulsion; in a military unit or prison, it may be threats, bodily harm, court-martial, or more recently "fragging."

The ability of the group to achieve conformity to its value system can be seen clearly in a set of classic studies conducted by Asch in the 1950's.[5] Student groups varying in size were instructed to match the length of a given line with one of three other lines, only one of which was the same size as the original. Each member of the group announced his judgments publicly. After a few trials, one member of the group found himself repeatedly contradicted (in 12 of the 18 trials in the experiment) by the other members. In fact the entire group, with the exception of this one critical subject, were "stooges" of the experimenter and were instructed to give a predetermined wrong answer. The single person, the critical subject, was placed in the position of a minority of one against a unanimous majority of his peers. In a sense he had two opposing forces impinging upon him—the evidence of his own eyes and the unanimous evidence of a group of equals. The data for 50 critical subjects can be seen in Table 7-1. Thirteen subjects were completely able to ignore the group and not conform. The majority of the subjects tended to make three or more "errors," that is, claimed that the correct line was the incorrect one the group had selected. Under control conditions in which

[5] Solomon E. Asch, "Effects of Group Pressure upon Modification and Distortion of Judgments," in *Readings in Social Psychology* (3rd ed.), eds. Eleanor E. Maccoby, Theodore M. Newcomb, and Eugene L. Hartley (New York: Holt, Rinehart & Winston, Inc., 1958), pp. 174-83.

TABLE 7-1   Distribution of Errors in Experimental and
Control Groups

Number of Critical Errors	Critical Group * (N = 50)	Control Group (N = 37)
	F	F
0	13	35
1	4	1
2	5	1
3	6	
4	3	
5	4	
6	1	
7	2	
8	5	
9	3	
10	3	
11	1	
12	0	
Total	50	37
Mean	3.84	0.08

* All errors in the critical group were in the direction of the majority estimates.
Source: H. Guetzkow, *Groups, Leadership and Men* (Carnegie-Mellon University: Carnegie Press, 1951).

no stooges were present, it can be seen that 35 of 37 subjects made no "errors" at all.

In a marketing context, Venkatesan conducted a similar experiment, in which subjects in groups of four were asked to choose the best of three identical men's suits. When three of the four group members were instructed by the experimenter to publicly choose a preselected suit, 22 of 42 critical subjects also chose that particular suit. When there was no group pressure, control groups selected the suits on a chance basis.[6]

Numerous studies have indicated the influence of the group upon the individual in changing his consumption patterns. For example, a study by Wellerman attempted to change eating habits of students from white bread to whole wheat bread. When the change was individually requested, the degree of eagerness to eat white bread varied greatly with the degree of personal preference for the food item; in the condition where the decision to change was made by the group, eagerness to consume whole wheat bread seemed to be relatively free of personal prefer-

[6] M. Venkatesan, "Experimental Study of Consumer Behavior Conformity and Independence," *Journal of Marketing Research*, Vol. 3 (November, 1966), 384-87.

ence.[7] Other experiments produced similar results. During World War II in the attempt to increase the consumption of beef hearts, sweetbreads, and kidneys and to reduce the consumption of the more desirable cuts of meat, one set of groups was given attractive lectures, concerned with the nutritional and economic value of these cuts, and was presented with recipes for their preparation. Other groups discussed among themselves the advantages and disadvantages of serving viscera. Follow-up studies indicated that 3 percent of the lecture group's and 32 percent of the discussion group's members began to prepare and serve these meats to their families.[8] Similar results have been found in increasing consumption of fresh milk, orange juice, cod-liver oil, and evaporated milk.[9] Further, these increases and the discrepancy between individual and group decisions were not short-term; follow-up studies indicated that the changes appeared to be permanent.

The Family Unit

Perhaps the single most influential group in the consumption behavior pattern of an individual is the family group. Without doubt, preferences for food items, life styles, and other relevant patterns have their roots in the primary family group. An examination of the family also immediately points out the concept of assigned roles within any group. Again, perhaps, role specialization can best be seen in a military unit with specialized roles assigned and differential behavior expected from officers, noncommissioned officers, gunners, ammunition carriers, etc. Within the family, role specialization is often equally obvious: the child has very clear limits on his behavior and influence; he may be allowed to suggest the brand of cereal consumed and perhaps the type of pet owned, but he has no direct say on the brand of battery bought for the family car or of deodorant for the medicine cabinet. Typically men have the roles of "bread-winner," and decision-maker on the purchase of tires, batteries, power lawn mowers, and perhaps power tools; women generally take the roles of cook, housekeeper, and decision-maker on household items. In addition, for most food items women have another role—that of the *gatekeeper*. In the home it is the housewife who chooses most products and most brands. Her decision may or may not be influenced by the likes and tastes of other family members, her guests, and perhaps even the neighborhood coffee club, but the control of the last gate in the channels of distribution from producer to consumer is in her hands. The husband may like strong coffee and the child sugared cornflakes, but it is she who makes the ultimate decision to purchase and it is she who selects the brand and size of package.

[7] Kurt Lewin, *Field Theory in Social Sciences: Selected Theoretical Papers* (New York: Harper & Row, Publishers, 1951).

[8] Kurt Lewin, "Group Decision and Social Change," in *Readings in Social Psychology,* eds. Maccoby, *et al., pp.* 297-311.

[9] Kurt Lewin, "Frontiers in Group Dynamics," *Human Relation,* Vol. 1 (1947), pp. 5-41.

The gatekeeper role can become particularly important in an industrial organization where the decision to purchase millions of dollars of supplies, machinery, computer hardware, and equipment may lie not in the hands of the board of directors or top management or even the ultimate user, but rather of the accountant or purchasing agent. However, within the family many decisions are not made unilaterally, but rather "the husband-wife dyad, or some combination of nuclear family members, is the decision-making unit." [10] For example, Wolgast has found that consumer decisions were most often made jointly between husband and wife, although one or the other tended to be dominant.[11] A study by Komarovsky indicated that joint involvement in decision-making is found to occur most in middle-income families and among younger couples and is related to the extent of husband-wife communication. Apparently among older married couples role specialization becomes more rigid.[12]

Perhaps the most thorough study of marital roles in consumer decision-making was carried out by Davis among 100 families living in four Chicago suburbs. Couples were asked a series of questions about the relative influence of husband and wife on the purchase of two durable goods—an automobile and living room furniture. Their responses can be found in Table 7-2.

A comparison of these two views reveals considerable variability in the husband-wife roles. It is also interesting to note that the perception of the wife and the perception of the husband differ as to who has the greater influence.[13]

FAMILY LIFE CYCLE

Although it is the family unit that purchases home appliances, toys, furniture, and garden appliances, this does not imply that all families are in the market at any one time or for that matter at any time.[14] For example, installment purchases are more frequent among young couples with children.[15] Several studies indicate that the purchase of china, silverware, drapes, slipcovers, retirement homes, and durables, in addition to homes and the more obvious baby furniture and toys, appear at different

---

[10] Thomas S. Robertson, *Consumer Behavior* (Glenview, Ill.: Scott-Foresman and Company, 1970), p. 75.

[11] E. H. Wolgast, "Do Husbands or Wives Make the Purchasing Decision?" *Journal of Marketing*, Vol. 23 (October, 1958), pp. 151-58.

[12] Mirra Komarovsky, "Class Differences in Family Decision Making," in *Consumer Behavior: Household Decision Making*, ed. Nelson N. Foote (New York: New York University Press, 1961), pp. 255-65.

[13] Harry L. Davis, "Dimensions of Marital Roles in Consumer Decision-Making," *Journal of Marketing Research*, Vol. 7 (May, 1970), 168-77.

[14] Perry Bliss, *Marketing Management and the Behavioral Environment* (Englewood Cliffs, N. J.: Prentice-Hall, Inc., 1970), p. 49.

[15] George Katona, *The Powerful Consumer* (New York: McGraw-Hill Book Co., 1960), p. 167.

TABLE 7-2   Marital Roles in Selected Automobile and Furniture Purchase Decisions as Perceived by Wives and Husbands
(N = 97)

Who decided:	Patterns of Influence (%) as Perceived by Wives			Patterns of Influence (%) as Perceived by Husbands		
	Husband has more influence than wife	Husband and wife have equal influence	Wife has more influence than husband	Husband has more influence than wife	Husband and wife have equal influence	Wife has more influence than husband
When to buy the automobile?	68	30	2	68	29	3
Where to buy the automobile?	59	39	2	62	35	3
How much to spend for the automobile?	62	34	4	62	37	1
What make of automobile to buy?	50	50	—	60	32	8
What model of automobile to buy?	47	52	1	41	50	9
What color of automobile to buy?	25	63	12	25	50	25
How much to spend for furniture?	17	63	20	22	47	31
When to buy the furniture?	18	52	30	16	45	39
Where to buy the furniture?	6	61	33	7	53	40
What furniture to buy?	4	52	44	3	33	64
What style of furniture to buy?	2	45	53	2	26	72
What color and fabric to select?	2	24	74	2	16	82

Source: Harry L. Davis, "Dimensions of Marital Roles in Consumer Decision-Making," *Journal of Marketing Research,* Vol. 7 (May, 1970), 168-77.

time periods within the family life cycle.[16] Hence, it appears that as the family grows older, roles become more specialized, the decision-making for any given product becomes more unilateral, and quite obviously the pattern of consumption and purchase changes.

[16] Bliss, *Marketing Management and the Behavioral Environment,* p. 49. See also Alan R. Andreasen, "Geographic Mobility and Market Segmentation," *Journal of Marketing Research,* Vol. 3 (November, 1966), 341-48; and William D. Wells and George Gubar, "The Life Cycle Concept in Marketing Research," *Journal of Marketing Research,* Vol. 3 (November, 1966), 355-63.

Reference Groups

For his protection, his enhancement, and his self-awareness, man needs others around him. Festinger claims that there exists in the human organism a drive to evaluate his opinions and his abilities; if objective nonsocial means are not available, people evaluate their opinions and abilities by comparison with the opinions and abilities of others.[17]

Herbert Hyman coined the term *reference group* to designate the type of group that an individual uses as a "point of reference" in determining his own judgments, preferences, beliefs, and behavior. In the limiting case, a reference group can be a single individual (although perhaps in this case the term *group* should not be used); in the other direction it can be a very large aggregate of persons, such as a political party, a social institution, or even a subculture or social class (although perhaps here, too, the term *group* is inappropriate). The individual may turn to the reference group in whole or only in part; he may or may not be a member of any particular reference group that is influencing him; or he may even use the group as a reference point in an entirely negative way.

Shibutani points out that current usage discloses three distinct referents for the single concept: [18]

(1) *Groups which serve as comparison points.* In the original usage by Hyman, the group is used as point of comparison in evaluating one's own status. Hyman had found that estimates of one's status varied according to the group with which the respondent compared himself. For example, the judgments of rear-echelon soldiers overseas concerning their fate varied, depending on whether they compared themselves to the soldiers still at home or those in combat. So, too, the feelings of affluence of the individual consumer varies, depending on whether he is comparing himself with his fellow man on the right or wrong side of the tracks.

(2) *Groups to which man aspires.* The reference group of the socially ambitious consists of people of higher strata whose status symbols are imitated. He aspires to membership in this reference group and imitates the behavior patterns of that group, including their buying behavior.

(3) *Groups whose perspectives are assumed by the individual.* This group's perspective constitutes the frame of reference for the individual; through direct or vicarious participation in a group he begins to perceive the world from its standpoint. Yet this group need not be one in which he aspires to membership. A member of a minority group may despise the white majority but still may see the world largely through its eyes. In this usage, a reference group can be real or imagined, envied or despised, but its perspective is assumed by the actor in any case.

There is little question that a reference group has the ability to exert enormous influence upon the individual. For example, the American As-

[17] Leon Festinger, "A Theory of Social Comparison Processes," *Human Relations,* Vol. 7 (May, 1954), 117-40.

[18] Tamotsu Shibutani, "Reference Groups as Perspectives," *American Journal of Sociology,* Vol. 60 (May, 1955), 562-69.

sociation of University Professors has from time to time censured colleges; a censure is often perceived as a blackball and many professors who hold the same value system as the AAUP, that is, who look upon the AAUP as a reference group, will not accept employment at censured institutions. Under these conditions, the AAUP functions as a *positive reference group;* the individual behaves in a manner congruent with the recommendations of the association. It is also conceivable that there may be rich industrialists who perceive all professors as communist-inspired dupes of left-wing revolutionaries. If, because of AAUP censure, these industrialists were to donate large amounts of money to the censured schools, the AAUP might function as a *negative reference group.* Another example of a negative reference group might be the individual who on election day purchases a despised newspaper and votes exactly the opposite of the printed recommendations, with the voiced opinion that what is good for this particular newspaper cannot be good for him.

For certain types of products and brands it should be apparent that reference group influence, positive or negative, should make a significant impact on consumer behavior. Bourne claims that the choice of both brand and product are influenced by reference groups in the case of cigarettes, beer, and cars. Whether one drinks beer or not and whether he drinks premium or regular is influenced by others. In the case of clothing, furniture, magazines, and refrigerators, Bourne states that reference groups are not influential in whether or not the product is used but are influential in the choice of brands. For still other products such as soap, canned peaches, and radios, reference groups are influential in the selection of neither the product nor the brand.[19] Unfortunately this is one of the many areas in consumer behavior in which very little research has been conducted, although the concept has a great deal of intuitive appeal and undoubtedly will be studied further in the coming years. The research which has been done, however, has shed light on the process of personal influence and opinion leadership.

Personal Influence and Opinion Leadership

For as long as books have been written about marketing or advertising, it has been clear that much occurs which affects consumer behavior other than those factors under the control of the marketer. It has often been said that "word-of-mouth advertising" has more influence on the success of the product than all the millions of dollars spent on advertising. This is no doubt true of some products and untrue of others, but until recently it was simply a matter of speculation: we did not know how to harness our knowledge about so widespread and difficult-to-measure a phenomenon as "word-of-mouth advertising." In recent years, we have been learning more because of the major contributions by Katz and Lazarsfeld to understanding the part played by people in the flow

[19] Francis S. Bourne, "Group Influences in Marketing and Public Relations," in *Perspectives in Consumer Behavior,* eds. Kassarjian and Robertson, pp. 289-96.

of mass communications.[20] Their investigation of personal influence (a broader and more useful term than "word-of-mouth") covered four areas of activity: (1) fashion, (2) movie-going, (3) public affairs (politics), and (4) marketing (which related primarily to brand choice).

THE TWO-STEP FLOW OF COMMUNICATION

The major finding of the original study was to substantiate the hypothesis that "the flow of mass communication may be less direct than was commonly supposed. [Rather] . . . influences stemming from the mass media first reach 'opinion leaders' who, in turn, pass on what they read and hear to those of their everyday associates for whom they are influential." [21] A number of studies found substantial support for the hypothesis in a variety of situations. As a result, further research in marketing has attempted to elaborate on the influence of opinion leaders (influentials) on others (influencees).

The *two-step flow thesis* says that communications are not all vertical, i.e., from the mass media down to the consumer; rather, there is a vertical step from the mass media to the opinion leader followed by a horizontal step from them to others. King tested the hypothesis against the then-popular belief that fashion adoption "trickled down" through the upper to lower levels of society; his results support the two-step flow thesis, and he suggests that the "trickle down" assumption be replaced by a "trickle across" one.[22] Additional support was presented in a study of group influence by Stafford: the leaders in small face-to-face groups influenced the level of brand loyalty and the brand choice of group members.[23]

All this, added to the substantiation of the thesis for "marketing" in the original study, has left the idea fairly well accepted among consumer researchers. The student should be very careful, however, in interpreting the words "leader" and "follower," or "influential" or "influencee." While this research does not indicate that we are a nation of sheep being herded around by the mass media, it does suggest that there might be a large number of "flocks of sheep" (groups) with their own "shepherd" (opinion leader). However, this is not accurate; the communication process has broad participation, as we shall see in the section which follows.

[20] Elihu Katz and Paul F. Lazarsfeld, *Personal Influence: The Part Played by People in the Flow of Mass Communications* (New York: The Free Press, 1955).

[21] Elihu Katz, "The Two-Step Flow of Communication: An Up-to-Date Report on an Hypothesis," *Public Opinion Quarterly*, Vol. 21 (Spring, 1957), 61-78.

[22] Charles W. King, "Fashion Adoption: A Rebuttal to the 'Trickle Down' Theory," in *Toward Scientific Marketing*, ed. Stephen A. Greyser (Chicago: American Marketing Association, 1964), pp. 108-25.

[23] James E. Stafford, "Effects of Group Influences on Consumer Brand Preferences," *Journal of Marketing Research*, Vol. 3 (February, 1966), 68-75. Less support for the phenomenon has been found in industrial markets: Frederick E. Webster, Jr., "Word-of-Mouth Communication and Opinion Leadership in Industrial Markets," in *Marketing and the New Science of Planning*, ed. Robert L. King (Chicago: American Marketing Association, 1968), pp. 455-59.

CHARACTERISTICS OF OPINION LEADERS

Who are the opinion leaders in marketing? The original study, which was limited in the number of characteristics it supplied, says that marketing leaders are found in about equal numbers in the various levels of social status (similar to King's finding with fashion). The two strongest factors setting marketing leaders apart are stage in the life cycle and gregariousness. Experience as a housewife, and presumably as a shopper, are important. Unmarried women are less likely to be leaders than women with small families, who are less likely to be leaders than women with large families. Apparently, *current* experience is the important thing, because matrons (women whose families are grown) score even lower than unmarried women. Within each of these classes, as well as in the entire group, the more gregarious women are, the more likely they were to be marketing leaders.[24]

Another characteristic of opinion leaders (in marketing and elsewhere) is their greater exposure to the media, particularly media in their area of leadership. An opinion leader is one whose advice is sought on the issue at hand. Perhaps this is because she is more knowledgeable than others because of this greater exposure, or because she feels obligated to "keep up" because her advice is sought; perhaps both are true. Also indicative of leadership is a tendency to deviate less from group norms —status is ascribed to the one who deviates least from the norms.[25]

There is evidence to support either a positive or negative answer to the question of whether or not opinion leaders are also innovators. Engel, Kegerreis, and Blackwell selected a particularly innovative new service, the automobile diagnostic center, as their indicator of innovativeness. They found that "[w]ithin a few days after trial, 90% had told at least one other person about it, and 40% had told two or more." [26] King, on the other hand, found that early adopters of fashion innovations were not the dominant personal influentials.[27] There is a great deal of difference between designated opinion leaders and someone who simply tells someone else about a new service, so differences in methods may explain these contradictory results. We will have to wait for further research to establish the connection between opinion leadership and innovativeness.

In short, rather than these somewhat general characteristics, "[o]pinion leaders and the people whom they influence are very much alike and typically belong to the same primary groups of families, friends and co-workers. While the opinion leader may be more interested in the par-

[24] See "Who Are the Marketing Leaders?" *Tide* (May 9, 1958), pp. 53-57.

[25] Everett M. Rogers and David G. Cartano, "Methods of Measuring Opinion Leadership," *Public Opinion Quarterly*, Vol. 26 (Fall, 1962), 435-41.

[26] James F. Engel, Robert J. Kegerreis, and Roger D. Blackwell, "Word-of-Mouth Communication by the Innovator," *Journal of Marketing*, Vol. 33 (July, 1969), 15-19.

[27] King, *Toward Scientific Marketing*, ed. Stephen A. Greyser, p. 119.

ticular sphere in which he is influential, it is highly unlikely that the persons influenced will be very far behind the leader in their level of interest. Influentials and influencees may exchange roles in different spheres of influence." [28] The most striking difference setting opinion leaders apart is their exposure to media relevant to their sphere of influence. The logical practical conclusion from this is that fashion marketers should advertise in fashion magazines, food marketers in women's magazines, furniture marketers in *Better Homes & Gardens* and *House Beautiful*, and so on. It will be important in future research to more clearly identify opinion leader characteristics so implications that are not redundant can be drawn.

OVERLAP OF OPINION LEADERSHIP

Another unsettled, but persistent, question concerns the existence of a "generalized" opinion leader. That is, is an opinion leader in one sphere likely to be an opinion leader in another? Katz and Lazarsfeld were interested in this question themselves and concluded that the hypothesis of a generalized leader was not supported by their research.[29] A subsequent rebuttal to their methods of testing the contention and to their conclusion showed that some statistically significant but practically unimportant overlap does exist.[30]

But even if there are not meaningful overlaps among leaders in such disparate spheres as fashion and public affairs, what about generalized *marketing* leaders? This more precise question would appear to elicit an easier answer than the first, but it does not. Here, even consumer researchers disagree with themselves (or their research does not supply consistent results). Robertson and Myers found little overlap in one project, and Myers and Robertson found "a number of significant overlaps of opinion leadership for closely-related categories." [31] Silk found no overlap in one study,[32] and in another, Montgomery and Silk found evidence "of significant amounts of overlap in opinion leadership across most but not all of the categories studied." [33] Finally, King and Summers found significant overlap of self-reported opinion leadership among a

---

[28] Katz, *Public Opinion Quarterly*, Vol. 21, p. 77.

[29] Katz and Lazarsfeld, *Personal Influence*, p. 334.

[30] Alan S. Marcus and Raymond A. Bauer, "Yes: There Are Generalized Opinion Leaders," *Public Opinion Quarterly*, Vol. 28 (Winter, 1964), 628-32.

[31] Reported in Robertson, *Consumer Behavior*, p. 87.

[32] Alvin J. Silk, "Overlap among Self-Designated Opinion Leaders: A Study of Selected Dental Products and Services," *Journal of Marketing Research*, Vol. 3 (August, 1966), 255-59.

[33] David B. Montgomery and Alvin J. Silk, "Patterns of Overlap in Opinion Leadership and Interest for Selected Categories of Purchasing Activity," in *Marketing Involvement in Society and the Economy*, ed. Philip R. McDonald (Chicago: American Marketing Association, 1969), pp. 377-86.

variety of product classes, with the highest overlap among product categories which involve similar interests.[34]

What should be clear from the above, as with the characteristics of opinion leaders, is that much research remains to be done before students of consumer behavior will be able to feel confident in the existence of a generalized opinion leader. The potential value of the entire issue of personal influence hopefully will prompt that research.

Summary

1. A group is not just any collection of people, but is "two or more people who bear an *explicit psychological relationship to each other.*" Two clarifying conditions are that a group consists of (a) persons who are interdependent upon each other such that each member's behavior potentially influences the behavior of each of the others, and (b) the sharing of an ideology—a set of beliefs, values, and norms—which regulates their mutual conduct.

2. The *structure* of a group varies, from formal relationships of authority (as within a military unit) to quite informal interpersonal relations (as in friendship circles).

3. For a group to survive, it must perform *functions* for its members. This may range from biological survival, as in the family group, to a sense of belonging or opportunity for socialization, as in a sorority.

4. For a group to continue in existence, it must exert *pressure* on the individual to *conform* to its ideology. Each group has enforcing agents, techniques, and sanctions for improper (deviant) behavior. These may range from subtle ridicule to actual expulsion from the group. The effect is to control the behavior of members, to make it conform to the group's ideals and norms.

5. Because of its critical importance to consumer behavior, the *family* group has been carefully investigated. Important information is available on the influence of children, husbands, wives, and joint influences on purchase decisions of various product classes.

6. A *reference group* is the type of group (or person or class) that the individual uses as a "point of reference" in determining his own judgments, preferences, beliefs, and behavior, which includes (a) groups which serve as *comparison points* (the Joneses with whom we compete), (b) groups to which man *aspires* (higher social classes), and (c) groups whose *perspectives are assumed by the individual* (vicarious group participation without belonging or aspiring to belong).

7. Groups influence consumers both in *whether or not* they use certain

---

[34] Charles W. King and John O. Summers, "Overlap of Opinion Leadership across Consumer Product Categories," *Journal of Marketing Research*, Vol. 7 (February, 1970), 43-50. See also an attack upon these conclusions and a rejoinder in Seymour Sudman, "Overlap of Opinion Leadership across Consumer Product Categories," *Journal of Marketing Research*, Vol. 8 (May, 1971), 258-59; and John O. Summers and Charles W. King, "Overlap of Opinion Leadership: A Reply," *Journal of Marketing Research*, Vol. 8 (May, 1971), 259-61.

product classes, and in *brand* choice. For some products (cigarettes, beer) *both* influences are present; for others (clothing, furniture, appliances) the group influences *only brand* choice; for still others (soup, canned peaches) reference groups are influential in the selection of *neither* the product nor the brand.

8. The importance of "word-of-mouth" advertising has been clarified by recent research. An important aspect has been the recognition and identification of *opinion leaders*. An important finding is that influence does not "trickle down" through society as was once presumed. Rather, there appears to be a *two-step-flow down* from the media to opinion leaders at all levels and then *across* to followers within strata.

9. Opinion leaders are characterized by many interpersonal contacts (gregariousness), and by above-normal exposure to media relevant to their sphere of influence.

10. The search for the "generalized" opinion leader (leadership overlapping in many spheres) has been illusive with conflicting evidence. Its importance to consumer behavior makes further study attractive.

8

CLASS
AND
CULTURE

The progression of this book so far has been from individual behavioral constructs, such as learning, perception, etc., through interpersonal group constructs. This chapter will deal with the behavioral constructs of larger aggregates of consumers and culture, previously defined by one theory as exogenous variables. That progression has been from the contributions of the psychologist, to those of the social psychologist, and now to those of the sociologist and cultural anthropologist.

Social Stratification

As we pointed out earlier, students of marketing have deservedly become disenchanted with purely economic explanations of consumer choice behavior. Income and price, though important, are not adequate for explaining differences in choice. As income in the United States has become more evenly distributed, more and more variation in consumption patterns exists *within* the same income groups. As society becomes more affluent and greater freedom of choice more evident, the disparity in choice patterns becomes exaggerated. This rising affluence has likewise reduced the importance of price as a determinant of choice. The sociologist's theories of social stratification have proved to be a fruitful source of explanation for these differences.

BASIS OF STRATIFICATION

It is a universal aspect of human societies that they are all socially stratified.[1] But what exactly do we mean by *social stratification?* Every

---

[1] For a discussion of the inability of even small subcultures to avoid social stratification, see the discussion of Israeli *kibbutzim* in Bernard Barber, *Social Stratification: A Comparative Analysis of Structure and Process* (New York: Harcourt, Brace

society has needs or functions that must be satisfied; for life to go on at all, certain functions or *roles* devolve on the society's members. Even in very simple or exotic societies, there exists some differentiation in these roles: while most male-adult roles may be "hunter-warrior," there is still a need for "chief" and "medicine man" roles. As societies become more advanced and complex, the role differentiation increases rapidly. All modern societies have a highly complex and highly differentiated set of roles. For social stratification to exist, however, these differentiated roles must be *valued* differently. Some roles must be more and some less highly valued by society's members. If "chief" and "hunter-warrior" are equally valued, no basis for stratification exists. In both primitive and modern societies, however, the differentiated roles are not equally valued. Even in the Soviet Union, where there is a deliberate effort to avoid social stratification, some roles are valued differently from others. One might argue that public health needs of the society make both "doctor" and "garbage collector" roles necessary; however, individual members of society are the ones who value the various roles, in this case usually valuing "doctor" higher than "garbage collector." These two characteristics of society—differentiation and evaluation—are the bases of social stratification.

It is evident to all but the most naive that the United States has a stratified society, that is, one in which there is *inequality*. In spite of the so-called "American Dream," the people that make up our society are not equal. All are not afforded the same power and prestige, do not have similar possessions, do not interact indiscriminately, and do not share the same value systems.[2] All occupations are not equally prestigious, and we are all at least partially conscious of class differences. There is some understanding that some individuals are "above" others and some "below" others socially. Everyone knows that there are some members of society with whom he is more "comfortable." In short, there is an ordering of individuals in society from high to low in terms of social status.

CLASS AND CASTE

Systems of social stratification can either be *closed* or *open* to social mobility. We often stereotype India as having a closed system of *castes:* an individual born into a particular caste must remain within that caste for his entire life; no opportunity for upward movement across caste

---

& World, 1957), pp. 12-16; for a fascinating dialogue of the functionality of this ubiquitous phenomenon, see the seven pieces reprinted in Reinhard Bendix and Seymour Martin Lipset, *Class, Status, and Power* (2nd ed.) (New York: The Free Press, 1966), pp. 47-72.

[2] For a brief introduction to the contributions of political science to consumer behavior in the sphere of power, prestige, values, and pressure groups see Perry Bliss, *Marketing Management and the Behavioral Sciences* (Englewood Cliffs, N. J.: Prentice-Hall, Inc., 1970), especially pages 105-21.

lines exists. Caste systems normally are maintained by some outwardly recognizable symbol, such as skin color. The black everywhere and the Mexican-American in the Southwest are examples of castes in United States' society. To some extent, they are permanently barred from upward social mobility; instead, they form subcultures with their own system of social stratification. Nevertheless, the general system of social stratification in the United States is more or less one of open *classes:* an individual is "born into" a class in that he becomes a member of the class to which his parents belong. However, there are possibilities for some social mobility for most individuals in this country, much of whose mythology is the often told story of "rags-to-riches." The son of an immigrant laborer fights his way to the presidency of a large corporation. Not only has this lad climbed the income ladder, he has also climbed the social class ladder.

A *social class* is a large number of individuals or families approximately equal to each other and differentiated from outsiders in terms of social status. It may be more accurate to think of a continuum of social status and prestige, but lumping groups together into classes is a useful and not inaccurate technique for describing the entire social system; there is, in fact, a tendency for individuals to group their fellows into classes. Social classes are less distinct than castes and are not as subject to analytical precision. Some values as well as some possessions are held in common by different classes. Mobility up or down may take place within as well as between generations; two of the factors that affect the amount of mobility are the degree of industrialization of the society as well as the degree of urbanization. Individuals in the United States typically move up the class structure through education, although other avenues may be available.

THE FACTORS AFFECTING CLASS PLACEMENT

There are a number of factors that can be used to place individuals in various social class systems, and there is considerable dispute about just which factors should be used. One source lists no less than twelve factors that have been used to make class placements: [3]

> authority
> power (political, economic, military)
> ownership of property, relation to the means of production,
>   control over land (the feudal estates)
> income (amount, type, and sources)
> consumption patterns and style of life
> occupation or skill, and achievement in it
> education, learning, wisdom
> divinity, "control" over the supernatural
> altruism, public service, morality

[3] Bernard Berelson and Gary A. Steiner, *Human Behavior: An Inventory of Scientific Findings* (New York: Harcourt, Brace & World, 1964), p. 454.

place in "high society," kinship connections, ancestry (i.e.,
 inherited position)
associational ties and connections
ethnic status, religion, race.

Any system of class placement normally includes a combination of a
number of these or other factors. What is important is that the factors
chosen should in some way reflect the values most highly prized by the
society; in a materialistic society, for instance, some consideration should
be given to income and ownership of property. In addition, the factors
chosen should be of relatively long-range duration and operational in
the sense that they can be measured. Further, they should lead to consistency in placement, and inconsistencies should be slight and infre-
quent. If occupation and income were to be used for placement, for
example, discrepancies would exist for high-income "bookies" and low-
income professors.

WARNER'S SIX-CLASS SYSTEM

Professor W. Lloyd Warner of the University of Chicago is largely responsible for the development of a system of social stratification that
has been widely used by both sociologists and students of consumer
behavior. This system, which divides United States' society into six
classes, was developed from investigations carried out in fairly small
cities, but subsequent use of the system in Chicago indicates that the
same classes exist in large cities as well. The following brief descriptions
of the six classes should prove adequate for our purposes.

1. *Upper-Upper.* The upper-upper class is very small, including less
than one percent of the population—the prominent, "social-register"
families with wealth inherited through two or more generations. The
members of this class have had the benefit of the "right" schools—Bryn
Mawr, Radcliffe, or Vassar for the women; Harvard, Princeton, or Yale
for the men. Their occupations include executive positions in the family
businesses, the various professions, or public service, as with Franklin
Roosevelt and Nelson Rockefeller. "The basic values of these people
might be summarized in these phrases: living graciously, upholding the
family reputation, reflecting the excellence of one's breeding, and dis-
playing a sense of community responsibility." [4]

2. *Lower-Upper.* The lower-upper class includes perhaps about two
percent of the population. Although these families are as wealthy or
more wealthy than the upper-upper class, their wealth is first generation. These nouveau riche are not fully accepted socially by the upper-
upper class nor accorded the prestige of old wealth by society in general.
Their children or grandchildren will go to the better schools, inherit

[4] Richard P. Coleman, "The Significance of Social Stratification in Selling,"
in *Marketing: A Maturing Discipline,* ed. Martin L. Bell (Proceedings of the American Marketing Association, December, 1960), pp. 171-84.

their wealth, and perhaps be accepted into the upper-upper class. The men in this class are highly successful business executives, doctors, lawyers, and owners of large businesses. They are highly motivated to give their children the same training in the social graces as is received by the upper-upper class, hopefully leading to social intercourse and perhaps intermarriage with that class.

3. *Upper-Middle.* The third-highest class in the social stratification system is much larger than the first two, comprised of about ten percent of the population. This group includes families with better-than-average incomes derived from a variety of sources: moderately successful business managers, doctors, dentists, lawyers, certified public accountants, college professors, and owners of medium-sized businesses. Their incomes are derived from salaries, profits, or professional fees, and their drive for professional success and membership in the upper classes is very strong. They attempt, as best they can with their limited incomes, to copy the lifestyle of the upper classes; these attempts are often reflected in clothing and home furnishings. "For most marketing and advertising purposes, this class and the two above it can be linked together into a single category of 'upper status people.' The major differences between them— particularly between the upper-middle and the lower-upper—are in degree of 'success' and the extent to which this has been translated into gracious living." [5] Almost all adults in this class have a college education.

4. *Lower-Middle.* The lower-middle class, comprising about one-third of the families in the society, is the first of the two really large classes. Occupations in this class include lower-level supervisors, nonmanagerial white-collar workers, owners of small (usually retail) businesses, bank clerks, insurance salesmen, large farm owners, teachers, etc. They place high value on respectability, participation in white-collar-dominated clubs, church attendance, and so forth, living in respectable white-collar neighborhoods, sending their children to college, and avoiding lower-class living. The importance of this class and the one below it (upper-lower) is so great that the value systems, as well as psychological and behavioral characteristics, of the two will be discussed later in greater detail.

5. *Upper-Lower.* This is the largest class of all, containing about forty percent of the population. The incomes of the families in this class are about the same as the lower-middle class, but the sources of these incomes is *wages* rather than salary. This group, often referred to as the "working class," includes skilled, semiskilled, and manual laborers: blue-collar, unionized factory or construction workers, small farm owners, barbers, firemen, policemen, beauty operators, retail sales clerks, etc. Unlike the lower-middle class, they tend not to use their incomes to strive for middle-class "respectability."

6. *Lower-Lower.* The bottom fifteen percent of the population comprises the lower-lower class, the lowest income class, whose members are often unemployed or underemployed and often on public relief. Those

---

[5] Coleman, *Marketing: A Maturing Discipline,* ed. Martin L. Bell, pp. 171-84.

who are employed are unskilled, usually uneducated, and are employed as day laborers, migrant farm laborers, janitors, scrubwomen, newsboys, and in similar low-income occupations. This class accounts for a large proportion of the juvenile delinquency and other crime and has only about seven or eight percent of the total national purchasing power.

WORKING CLASS AND MIDDLE CLASS: PSYCHOLOGICAL AND BEHAVIORAL DIFFERENCES

The major contribution of the study of social stratification to our understanding of consumer behavior lies in its use as a means of segmenting the market into meaningful customer groups.[6] The stratification system used here adds little to this segmentation process beyond what could be accomplished by using income classes as relates to the upper and lower extremes. The two upper classes are also those with the highest incomes and wealth; the lower-lower class is also the lowest income class. These classes are of limited marketing significance, either because they are so small or because their incomes are limited; the great bulk of the people form the middle income brackets. A variety of historical factors, including the labor union movement, have worked to make these income brackets indistinguishable by social class. Many of the middle classes have incomes above those of the working class (upper-lower), but in many cases the reverse is true. This more even distribution of income, and especially the improvement in the lot of the working class, has made the task of market segmentation on the basis of income alone almost impossible, and certainly less meaningful.

In order to capture something of the flavor of the differences between the two largest social classes, a brief review of four aspects of their lifestyles will be of value: (1) the general view of the world, (2) the relationship between husband and wife, (3) the relationship between mother and child, and (4) the relationships among relatives. The lifestyle of the wives in these classes is most instructive, as they are the principal consumers.[7]

GENERAL WORLD VIEW

Compared to the middle class wife, the wife of the working class sees the world outside her home as somewhat threatening—something over which she has no control or real influence. As a result, she is passive:

---

[6] A fairly recent excellent review is James M. Carman, *The Application of Social Class in Market Segmentation* (University of California, Berkeley: IBER Special Publications, 1965).

[7] Much of the following is based on Lee Rainwater, Richard P. Coleman, and Gerald Handel, *Workingman's Wife: Her Personality, World and Life Style* (New York: Oceana Publications, Inc., 1959). The serious student of consumer behavior should read the work in its entirety, realizing that it is somewhat dated.

she rarely participates in activities outside the home, devoting much of her life to caring for her home, her children, and her husband. The middle class wife, on the other hand, is active. She is a "joiner," and takes part in affairs outside the home, largely because she believes she *can* influence the external world and does not see it as threatening. "The middle class woman experiences more variety in her life, and less monotony, because she has a much greater number of personal, avocational, and outside interests than does the working class wife." [8]

HUSBAND-WIFE RELATIONSHIPS

The most important interpersonal relationship for both working and middle class women is with their husbands, but the character of this relationship varies. To begin with, the beginning of this relationship usually comes earlier for the working class, who typically marry earlier, often immediately after graduation from high school. The middle class couple is more likely to have spent some years maturing, often in a college environment.

The working class wife is much more submissive, largely because of a greater sense of dependency. "Women's Lib" is almost totally a middle class (mostly upper-middle class) phenomenon. The writers of the TV show, "All in the Family," are true to Archie's working class status in his relation to his "ding-bat" wife. Men are supposed to be dominant and controlling, a carryover from earlier relationships with men, including her father. Husbands are just as important in the affection of middle class women, but they are much more confident about their relationships with their husbands. The middle class wife suffers much less anxiety and fear of losing her husband's affections. As a result, she is less willing to sacrifice her own wishes to please her husband. On the contrary, she is more apt to take an active role in shaping her husband's behavior. In the play *My Fair Lady*, Henry Higgins laments that once you marry a woman, "she goes on to the enthralling job of overhauling you," a typically middle class, not working class, wife's action.

Another aspect of the husband-wife relationship that is different between the middle and working class is that in the latter, the roles, the expected activities, are more clearly and distinctly demarcated. There is less "togetherness" in day-to-day activities. In the working class family, the work around the house is often separated between outside, the husband's responsibility, and the inside, the wife's. Middle class couples are more apt to share responsibility for chores; it is easier to get an apron on a middle class husband. The same holds true for recreational activities. The working class husband is more likely to engage in separate activities at the bar or bowling alley and even a separate vacation, such as hunting or fishing. The middle class husband might also spend some vacation time hunting or fishing, but his vacation nearly always includes time spent with his wife.

[8] Rainwater, *et al.*, *Workingman's Wife*, p. 34.

MOTHER-CHILD RELATIONSHIPS

In their relations with their children, working and middle class mothers have some similarities as well as some differences. Both are highly child-centered and emotionally involved in the child-rearing process. Children are the fulfillment of themselves and proof to the outside world of their worth. These feelings are, however, stronger in the working class women. They are much more protective of their children, for the world is, as we have seen, a potentially dangerous place. Middle class mothers are more matter-of-fact in sheltering their children.

Working class mothers look to their children for immediate gratification, while middle class mothers tend to look to the future. This leads to a tendency for one to enjoy spending for her children now, and for the other to save for her children's education. "The difference between middle and lower class mothers in their approach toward their children is nicely reflected in the fact that the latter relate to their children with 'gifts' hoping for a reciprocal gift of their affection, while the middle class women guide their children with goals, seeking the satisfactions attendant upon their realization." [9]

Social class clearly influences mothers' attitudes toward their children's education. Reflecting her own experiences, the working class mother doubts the real importance of school. Some working class mothers do want their children to be upwardly mobile, hoping that they will enter the middle classes, and they realize that education is the best means to this end; most, however, do not think that a working class life for their children is so bad and thinking thus train them for it. The middle class mother, on the other hand, strongly desires that her children retain their middle class standing or aspire to upward mobility. Education, therefore, is a necessity! The lack of education is real danger that can lead to the awful consequence of a working class existence for the child. She is concerned about the quality of the child's education and its ability to prepare the child for college, and she is also concerned with the social value of the school—that it have the "right" kind of companions for her child to associate with. Being sure of this "right" school is, in fact, one of the major factors involved in the purchase of a home in the right location.

FRIENDS AND RELATIVES

The working class woman reflects her fear of the "outside" world in her relations with people outside the immediate family as well as she does with her husband and children. Her friends are quite often relatives; although mothers and sisters are often her best friends, her whole circle of friendship relations is apt to include aunts, uncles, cousins, and in-laws. When asked what people outside the immediate family they saw the

[9] Rainwater, *et al.*, *Workingman's Wife*, p. 98.

most of, about one-half of the people mentioned by the working class women were relatives. The same question asked of middle class women resulted in a figure of about one-fifth. Over three-fourths of the working class included one or more relatives on their list of close friends, but only one-third of the middle class included any relatives at all. The working class woman feels more comfortable around her relatives and has more in common with them. It is not that she is antisocial or dislikes outsiders—she is afraid of them, afraid that they will not be interested in her. She doubts her worth.

Marriage does not signal the breaking of ties with mothers as much in the working class as in the middle class. The middle class woman is emancipated from her parents and seeks friends from a variety of sources. She participates more in the outside world, as we have said, and has many more opportunities for and is comfortable in making friends with outsiders. The personal friendship ties that consumers enjoy can strongly affect their buying behavior (see Chapter 7), and the objects of those ties thus take on special importance.

SOCIAL CLASS AND CONSUMER BEHAVIOR

Much of the previous discussion of the American class structure and of the differences in attitudes and behavioral patterns among the various classes may not appear to be directly related to consumption behavior. Attitudes toward child-rearing, however, may have strong implications, especially as relates to certain classes of products. Our purpose in this section is to answer the more specific question: how do class differences affect people's consumption behavior? Studies have shed considerable light on the issue and research is being done continuously, but much remains to be learned.

One very important aspect of consumer choice behavior that is affected by social class is that of the general priorities and preferences people show. What is important to the different classes? Working class women, very much tied to their homes, place considerable priority on spending on the home, especially on certain rooms. The kitchen is not only the major workplace of the working class wife, it is also the room in which she does a great deal of her "entertaining" of relative-friends. She places high priority, therefore, on spending on appliances and tools for the kitchen; a well-equipped workroom is as important to her as is the living room (the room that the outside world sees most) to the middle class wife. In addition, the working class mother spends a great deal on her children, often indulging them; she places high priority on the children's rooms in the house, often spending a great deal making them pretty.

The middle class woman, on the other hand, places higher priorities on the external and visible evidence of her consumption. She is somewhat guilty of "conspicuous consumption," though not so much so as are the upper classes. The living room is the center of the entertainment of work associates and other friends, and therefore gets a high priority. The furniture in this room is often a great deal more expensive and is almost always more tasteful than the furniture in the working class living room. The middle class family will forego the benefit of buying matched suites of furniture, which they could do if they were willing to settle for cheaper furniture, instead buying one good piece at a time in order to have furniture that they are sure will be approved by their peers. Middle class women are at least familiar with furniture styles, and their buying reflects this fact. Working class women, on the other hand, are rarely able to articulate their preferences for furniture. They do not know about styles and tend to prefer the "modern," which means the latest mass-produced style.

Social Research, Inc., of Chicago has utilized social class in the study of a great many categories of products. While all of these results are not publicly available, a participant has made reference to reports on a wide variety of products, including baby care products, women's clothing, men's clothing, telephones, feminine hygiene products, tampons, toothpaste, personal cleaning products, hair care products, chewing gum, laxatives and antacids, and food.[10] It is not important here to elaborate on the specific differences for these various product classes. What *is* important is that social class has been found to be a useful method for segmenting markets across a broad range of product classes. In some instances, however, it may not be important; purchases of air conditioners in the arid Southwest, for instance, is better explained by differences in income than in social class.[11]

One of the earliest studies of the impact of social class on consumer behavior dealt with its effect on *store choice* or shopping behavior. Shoppers in the various strata seek out retail outlets that reflect and cater to their particular class. "In a study of department stores and shopping behavior, it was found that the lower-status woman is completely aware that, if she goes into high-status department stores, the clerks and the other customers in the store will punish her in various subtle ways." [12] As a result, lower-status people are as anxious to avoid the upper class stores as the upper classes are to avoid the lower-status stores. What results is a retail structure that carries social class or social prestige characteristics. These differences are, of course, relative and are more noticeable with some classes of products than with others. The middle class shopper may be willing to buy products such as refrigerators or washing machines at discount houses, where "just anyone" may shop; with these items, the brand name is the assurance of quality. Where style or taste is important, as with furniture or clothing, the "right" store is very important to the middle class consumer.

[10] Sidney J. Levy, "Social Class and Consumer Behavior," in *On Knowing the Consumer*, ed. Joseph W. Newman (New York: John Wiley & Sons, Inc., 1966), pp. 146-60.

[11] Coleman, *Marketing: A Maturing Discipline*, ed. Martin L. Bell, pp. 171-84.

[12] Pierre Martineau, "Social Classes and Spending Behavior," *Journal of Marketing*, Vol. 23 (October, 1958), 121-30.

Some specific and important differences in preferences should be noted. The working class, for instance, tends to prefer the neighborhood store and generally shows a narrowness in store choice. They fear the dangers of going outside the neighborhood where one might be snubbed or ignored. These shoppers often avoid the downtown merchant and the large shopping centers. The middle class shopper is willing to shop in more places and has a wider range of possibilities.

In a study of cosmetics purchase behavior, it was found that upper-middle class women are apt to buy in department stores, lower class women prefer the variety store, and drugstores were about equally attractive to all.[13] When the classes do buy in the same store, they are likely to be after different items. When the working class woman shops in a particular store where the middle class woman buys most of her clothing and a number of other products, she is interested only in gifts. She invades the middle class world to buy gifts for others but not clothes for herself.

Another aspect of marketing behavior related to social class is that of the exposure of individuals to advertising media. If class is an important variable in segmenting the market, the various media are helpful in reaching these different market segments. Some of the most obvious differences are in exposure to various magazines. Magazines that carry a large number of emotional stories, such as *True Story,* are most likely to be found in the working class homes. Many of the "house and garden" variety of magazine, such as *House Beautiful,* are more likely to be read by the middle classes. Some magazines, such as *New Yorker,* are almost exclusively read by the upper and upper-middle classes. Most magazines make periodic reader studies, and the advertiser should know the social class the medium is reaching before using it.

Less subtle, but just as important, are the differences in television viewing by the various classes. "Analysis of program selection by social class revealed that the working class preferred known performers, and plots without much subtlety or psychological complications. The lower-middle class sought lively and absorbing programs, such as adventures and westerns. The upper-middle class criticized television programming in general and exercised discrimination in viewing."[14] The sex and social-class characteristics of program selection are summarized in Figure 8-1. The brand of humor, the style of storytelling, the socioeconomic situation of the participants on the show, and a number of other factors may make the show more in keeping with the attitudes and values of one class than another. Take, for example, the differences between two very popular comedy shows during the middle and late 1960's, "The Dick Van Dyke Show" and "The Honeymooners" with Jackie Gleason and Art

[13] Levy, *On Knowing the Consumer,* ed. Joseph W. Newman, p. 153.
[14] Harold H. Kassarjian and Thomas S. Robertson, *Perspectives in Consumer Behavior* (Glenview, Ill.: Scott-Foresman and Company, 1968), p. 375; based on the research of I. O. Glick and S. J. Levy, *Living with Television* (Aldine, 1962).

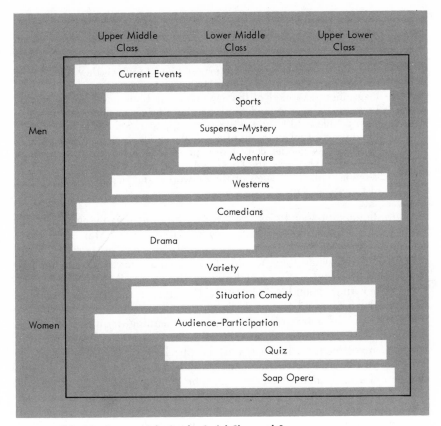

FIG. 8-1 Program Selection by Social Class and Sex

Carney. Dick Van Dyke is a writer for a television comic, clearly a middle class job. His home, where much of the action takes place, is typically middle class. He dresses in a suit outside the home and a sweater and tie at home. Jackie Gleason, on the other hand, is a bus driver—obviously working class. His best friend works for the sewage authority. He never wears a tie unless it is the bow tie part of his bus driver's uniform. His home is spare at best. The Dick Van Dyke humor is urbane, often subtle. The humor used by Jackie Gleason is much louder, coarser, more obvious, and often pure slapstick. These two comedy programs appear to reach different audiences, which could perhaps be largely explained in terms of social stratification.

The following quotation sums up many of the differences among the classes in their media choice behavior:

> The different meanings of media have been explored in many studies. The media function in varied ways, and each also fits differentially into the lives of the social classes. There are (sometimes

sharp) class preferences among the newspapers available in a community, in evaluating magazines, in selecting television shows, in listening to the radio, in how newspapers are read, in receipt and meaning of direct mail; and, in general, in the total volume of materials to which people are exposed and to which they attend in one or another of the media. Higher status people see more magazines, read more of the newspaper, and buy more newspapers. Lower class people tend to prefer the afternoon paper; middle class people tend to prefer the morning paper. Studies in the past three years of television in fifteen major cities show that upper middle class people consistently prefer the NBC channel, while lower middles prefer the CBS; and these preferences are in keeping with the images of the networks, and the characteristics of the social classes.[15]

The influence of social class on both saving and borrowing money has been subjected to analysis. In his early classic study, Martineau asked people to suppose their incomes were doubled over the next ten years, and to explain what they would do with that increased income. He found that the higher the social status, the more likely people are to save rather than spend.[16] "Moreover the higher the status, the more likely is the individual to specify *how* he will save his money, which is indicative of the more elaborate financial leaning required of higher status." [17] The lower the social class, the less likely the individual is to consider investment savings such as the purchase of stocks or insurance. The lower classes prefer the more tangible investments such as real estate, a farm, a small business, etc. The middle class respondents, on the other hand, preferred the investment outlets of stocks, insurance, etc.

In more recent research, Mathews and Slocum have shed some light on differences in the use of credit by the different classes. They studied the influence of class on the use of bank credit cards, such as "Master Charge" or "BankAmericard." They defined one use as *convenience*, which would be indicated if the individual used his card during the month to make credit purchases instead of paying cash, but then paid the balance within the billing cycle. If, on the other hand, the cardholder elected to pay only part of the billed amount and to pay interest on the balance, he was considered to be using it for *installment* purposes. They found very strong evidence that the lower the social class the greater the tendency to use bank credit cards for installment purposes, while the higher classes were more apt to use them for convenience.[18] Their study supported previous work that showed that the higher classes were better able to defer gratification or renounce impulses, while the lower classes tended to follow their impulses and had greater trouble in deferring

[15] Levy, *On Knowing the Consumer*, ed. Joseph W. Newman, pp. 155-56.
[16] Pierre Martineau, "Social Classes and Spending Behavior," *Journal of Marketing*, Vol. 23 (October, 1958), 121-30.
[17] Martineau, *Journal of Marketing*, Vol. 23, pp. 121-30.
[18] H. Lee Mathews and John W. Slocum, Jr., "Social Class and Commercial Bank Credit Card Usage," *Journal of Marketing*, Vol. 33 (January, 1969), 71-78.

gratification.[19] For public policy decisions, this research provides excellent support for the rationale that led to the prohibition on mailing out credit cards unsolicited.

Culture

Beginning with the third chapter, we have moved from consideration of individual difference constructs toward higher and higher levels of aggregation. This movement is indicative of the vantage points from which the various disciplines study human behavior—from psychology to social psychology to sociology and now to cultural anthropology. It should come as no surprise, then, to learn that much of what we have found useful in the study of consumer behavior earlier carries over here. Especially helpful is the material dealing with reference groups and group influence. The culture in which we live is much like a large impersonal reference group, as we shall see.

The concept *culture* is supple enough for us to stretch it to cover a wide spectrum of aggregation. We can speak of "Western culture" and include large portions of the modern world. It is equally legitimate to speak of a national (United States) or tribal (Hopi) culture. At its heart, the concept includes a set of *learned* beliefs, values, attitudes, habits, and forms of behavior that are *shared* by a society and are *transmitted* from generation to generation within that society.[20]

Much of Western culture holds a shared set of values and beliefs rooted in the Judeo-Christian heritage. One can find much of the teaching of the Old and New Testament writers as part of the value system (or even the law) of many Western European and North and South American nations. These shared values are what permit us to refer to a Western culture, to distinguish its members from the rest of the world. When we extend some of those values to "work is good," "God rewards frugality," and other beliefs which form what we know as the "Protestant ethic," we find that we share them with fewer peoples. These values are not shared by most southern Europeans, Latin Americans, or French-Canadians. It may be legitimate to refer to the Protestant ethic as a cluster of values and beliefs shared by the U. S. culture, but not appropriate in relation to the Western culture.

The beliefs, values, attitudes, habits, and forms of behavior refer to a wide range of concerns—many of which we simply take for granted. They include customs (use of eating utensils) and folkways (wearing a suit to church), which are not of serious concern to the society, but are be-

[19] For example, see Murray S. Straus, "Deferred Gratification, Social Class, and the Achievement Syndrome," *American Sociological Review*, Vol. 27 (June, 1962), 325-35; and A. Davis and J. Dollard, *Children of Bondage* (Washington, D. C.: American Council on Education, 1948).

[20] For more definitions than you would care to remember, see Alfred L. Kroeber and Clyde Kluckhohn, "Culture: A Critical Review of Concepts and Definitions," *Papers of the Peabody Museum*, 47, No. 1a (1952). For a lucid exposition, see Clyde Kluckhohn, "Culture and Behavior," in *Handbook of Social Psychology*, Vol. II, ed. Gardner Lindzey (Reading, Mass.: Addison-Wesley, 1954), pp. 921-76.

havioral norms. They also include mores, or fairly strong cultural norms (respect for elders, patriotism, heterosexuality), which are likely to elicit moral condemnation when violated. When a more becomes very important to a society, it may be codified in legal form. Mores which were once laws involved the use of alcohol and marriage between members of different races; mores which still are laws involve the use of marijuana and marriage between members of the same sex.

Just as with the norms of smaller groups, cultural norms are effective when they become internalized by the individual. The process by which this is done is known as *acculturation* when learning a culture of which one is not native, and *socialization* when learning one's native culture. Recall the discussion of the development of attitudes and the reference to the song "Carefully Taught" from *South Pacific*. Rodgers and Hammerstein were trying to say that the child will not grow up to hate "people whose eyes are oddly made, and people whose skin is a different shade," unless he is "carefully taught," i.e., socialized. That is why our definition of culture emphasizes the fact that these are *learned* beliefs, values, attitudes, habits, and forms of behavior. And, as with these examples, many values, attitudes, forms of behavior, etc., must "be taught before it's too late, before you are six or seven or eight."

The process of rewarding normative behavior and punishing deviant behavior (discussed in the preceding chapter) is the mechanism of the socialization and acculturation processes. Just as small primary (face-to-face) groups can punish deviant behavior through such acts as ostracizing the deviate, society in general can punish nonconformers in a variety of ways: we can stare at the fellow who eats peas from a knife, simply making him uncomfortable; we can ostracize the fellow with homosexual tendencies and bar him from certain jobs; and we can execute the fellow who violates society's norm, "Thou shalt not kill."

The society's literature, movies, political speeches, and even advertisements are all useful techniques for transmitting its culture, although the family is the principal means. Society often condemns the parent for the deviant behavior of the child, saying, "You have not done an adequate job of socialization." In parents' efforts to save their children from pot or premarital sex, the question "What will my friends think of me?" is often as important as "What harm will this do my child?"

SUBCULTURES

Melting pots rarely provide perfect homogeneity in their content, so we find subcultures within a society, which involve sets of *learned* beliefs, values, attitudes, habits, and forms of behavior that are *shared* by subsets of a society and are *transmitted* from generation to generation within each subset. Members of subcultures typically conform to many of the norms of the dominant culture, and deviate from others which are not compatible with norms of their subculture.

There are a number of dimensions upon which subcultures are based.

Some are based on *nationality*, as with the Italian-American [21] or Mexican-American subcultures or the French-Canadian subculture, which has become so deviant as to lead to a separatist movement. *Religion* is often the basis for subcultures: the Amish in the United States, the Catholic minority in Northern Ireland, and Orthodox Jews in many nations are examples of such subcultures. By far the most prominent subculture in the U. S. is based on *race*, and it is not surprising that it has received considerable attention by consumer researchers—as we shall see.

CULTURE IN CONSUMER BEHAVIOR

You will recall from the first chapter that culture is an *exogenous* variable, exerting influence on consumer behavior, including the principal "output" variable—purchase—through such constructs as attitudes, perceptual bias, and so on. The observable evidence of these effects are in (1) consumption differences, (2) preferences for media and messages, and (3) the pervasive, if obvious, effects on international marketing.

Consumption Differences. Many of the differences in consumption patterns among various subcultures center around food preferences and are too obvious to belabor here. Examples of the use of various kosher products by the Jewish subculture, of special foods (including a variety of pastas) among Italian-Americans, and of hominy grits and ham-hocks and butter beans in the South. Clothing styles are part of the belief structure of the Amish. Cultural taboos make the use of tobacco, liquor, and even coffee, tea, and soft drinks practically nonexistent among Mormons.[22]

The importance of the black subculture in the United States has led to a significant amount of research,[23] and it would be useful to begin with a view of general differences in black-white consumption patterns, depicted in Table 8-1.[24] A major category in which blacks spend less is housing, which is partially a function of noncompliance with "fair housing" laws. Together with spending less on other categories, blacks have

[21] Herbert J. Gans, *The Urban Villagers* (New York: The Free Press, 1962).

[22] For additional examples, see Milton Alexander, "The Significance of Ethnic Groups in Marketing New-Type Packaged Foods in Greater New York," in *Advancing Marketing Efficiency*, ed. Lynn H. Stockman (Chicago: American Marketing Association, 1959), pp. 557-61.

[23] Much of what follows is based on Raymond A. Bauer, "Negro Consumer Behavior," in *On Knowing the Consumer*, ed. Joseph W. Newman (New York: John Wiley & Sons, Inc., 1966), pp. 161-65; Raymond A. Bauer, Scott M. Cunningham, and Lawrence H. Wortzel, "The Marketing Dilemma of Negroes," *Journal of Marketing*, Vol. 29 (July, 1965), 1-6; and Charles E. Van Tassel, "The Negro as a Consumer— What We Know and What We Need to Know," in *Marketing for Tomorrow . . . Today*, eds. M. S. Mayer and E. S. Vosburgh (Chicago: American Marketing Association, 1967), pp. 166-68.

[24] The table is from Bauer, Cunningham, and Wortzel, *Journal of Marketing*, Vol. 29, pp. 1-6, but is based on data from Marcus Alexis, "Some Negro-White Differences in Consumption," *American Journal of Economics and Sociology*, Vol. 21 (January, 1962), 11-28.

TABLE 8-1   Black Spending Versus White Spending Behavior Controlled by Income

Food	Less
Housing	Less
Clothing	More
Recreation and leisure	Mixed
Home furnishings	More
Medical	Less
Auto transportation	Less
Non-auto	More
Savings	More
Insurance	Less

more to spend on certain discretionary items than do whites with comparable incomes.

While there is some debate over the issue, it is generally concluded that Negroes do use white norms as a guide to expenditures which will provide status in the dominant culture.[25] This helps explain findings that blacks purchase the status liquor—Scotch—and the best brands. They also spend much more on such items as men's shoes, purchasing more frequently and in better quality.

Advertising Media and Messages. As with social classes, subcultures may be attracted to particular media often designed for that specific group. "It has been established that radio is the major medium for Negroes, followed by television, newspapers, and magazines. And this pattern is known to be different than that for whites." [26]

Message strategy in advertising is affected by attitudes of subcultures. One such concern has been with the use of black models in advertisements. Barban and Cundiff found very little difference in reactions by Negro and white subjects to integrated and segregated advertisements under a number of media alternatives.[27] In a controlled experiment, Tongberg found essentially the same results, with perhaps some negative reaction of whites in lower social strata to ads containing black models.[28] A recent study suggests that the use of black models in ads is noticed

[25] Bauer, *op. cit.;* Bauer, Cunningham, and Wortzel, *op. cit.;* and Van Tassel, *op. cit.* It may be well to treat these conclusions with caution. Culture does change, and younger blacks may have adopted white middle class values in fewer numbers than have their elders.

[26] Van Tassel, *Marketing for Tomorrow . . . Today,* ed. M. S. Mayer and E. S. Vosburgh, p. 167.

[27] Arnold Barban and Edward Cundiff, "Negro and White Responses to Advertising Stimuli," *Journal of Marketing Research* (November, 1964), pp. 53-56.

[28] Richard Tongberg, "The Effect of Social Class and the Attitudes of Young Adults toward the Use of Negroes in American Advertising" (Unpublished working paper, The Pennsylvania State University, November 18, 1968).

by and favorably reacted to by blacks. Whites tend not to notice and are not affected when they do.[29]

Kassarjian studied the actual use of Negro models in magazine advertising over a 20-year period.[30] Using the years 1946, 1956, and 1965 for twelve popular magazines, he conducted a detailed content analysis of the frequency of use, the role, the racial make-up, and the kind of interaction (social, work, etc.) between persons in the ads. He found striking changes in the occupational roles of Negroes used in ads. "In 1946, 78 percent of American Negro actors or models were depicted in the ads as having laborer or service jobs: maid, waiter, slave, field hand, personal servant, the Aunt Jemima, or the Uncle Tom."[31] That figure had dropped to 13 percent by 1965, when nearly 60 percent were in sports or entertainment roles. In the ads with both white and black models, the relationships shifted from a predominance of superior-white–inferior-black in 1946, to a predominance of a peer relationship. In short, by 1965 advertising had made some strides away from representation of Negroes in servant/inferior stereotypes toward one of equality in roles.

Other subcultures are experiencing similar impact on advertising. The Frito-Lay company, after receiving pleas, demands, and ultimately legal action, stopped using their cartoon character "Frito Bandito" in their advertising. Similarly, Polish-American groups have gone so far as to use legal means to banish ethnic humor from advertising. Concern for the norms of subcultures, for such a simple notion, appears to be difficult for advertisers to learn.

International Marketing. The influence of culture on differences in consumer behavior in many countries is both obvious and ubiquitous. There is literally no activity, whether it is the shopping habits of the consumer or the pricing practices of the marketer, which is not influenced by the cultural differences among nations. It is not possible to catalog here the various effects of these cultural differences, so a few examples must suffice. French housewives consider the process of shopping in neighborhood stores where they are known and know the other patrons a social activity and resist giving it up for perhaps more "efficient" supermarkets. Latin Americans are likely to place more value on personal trust and friendship for business dealings than on faith in institutions.[32] In some Catholic and Latin countries, excessive care of the body is considered immoral; for this reason about eighty percent of French women use laundry soap instead of toilet soap for personal care.[33]

[29] Stuart Tolley and John J. Goett, "Reactions to Blacks in Newspaper Ads," *Journal of Advertising Research,* Vol. 11 (April, 1971), 11-17.

[30] Harold H. Kassarjian, "The Negro and American Advertising, 1946-1965," *Journal of Marketing Research,* Vol. 6 (February, 1969), 29-39.

[31] Kassarjian, *Journal of Marketing Research,* Vol. 6, p. 35.

[32] Edward T. Hall, "The Silent Language in Overseas Business," *Harvard Business Review,* Vol. 38 (May-June, 1960), 87-96.

[33] Ernest Dichter, "The World Customer," *Harvard Business Review,* Vol. 40 (July-August, 1962), pp. 113-22.

A CONCLUDING NOTE

The student of consumer behavior must retain one critical truth about culture. He, like everyone else, is a product of *his* culture. He has been socialized; he has internalized the norms of the dominant culture and perhaps of one or more subcultures. Without conscious effort, he will be aware of his own internalized norms. In creating some marketing communication, for instance, he will avoid violating those norms. On the other hand, he must study and consciously avoid the violation of the norms of other subcultures (domestic) or cultures (international) when preparing marketing communications.

Summary

1. *Social stratification* is universal. This is so because within any society (1) there is a variety of different functions or *roles* that must be performed, and (2) these different roles are *valued* differently by society's members themselves.

2. Sociologists have utilized a large number of variables as the basis for defining social classes, with occupation, education, and associational ties of special importance.

3. The six-class system of social stratification developed by Warner has been particularly useful to many sociologists and marketing researchers. This system is based on occupation, source of income, house type, and neighborhood.

4. In the study of consumer behavior, the major concern is with the middle class and working class. Women in the working class, in contrast to the middle class, are (a) more passive and view the world outside their home as threatening, (b) carry their passive role over into relations with their husbands, (c) are more protective of and receive more immediate gratification from their children, and (d) are more likely to list relatives (sisters, cousins, etc.) as their closest friends.

5. Social class differences have been useful in explaining differences in consumer behavior as relates to (a) preferences for products and brands, (b) store choice or shopping behavior, (c) exposure to advertising media, and (d) saving and the use of credit.

6. *Culture* involves a set of *learned* beliefs, values, attitudes, habits, and forms of behavior that are *shared* by a society, and are *transmitted* from generation to generation within that society.

7. Culture is maintained by society's transmission of customs, folkways, and mores through the process of *acculturation* and *socialization*. These processes are similar to those employed by small groups in insuring normative behavior of members.

8. *Subcultures* exist within the dominant culture and maintain their own set of beliefs, values, attitudes, habits, and forms of behavior. In the United States, the major bases of subcultures are nationality, religion, and race.

9. The largest U. S. subculture, that of *blacks,* has been studied in some detail by consumer researchers. Differences from the dominant white culture have been found in this group's (1) expenditures for a number of classes of products, and (2) their preferences for advertising media.

10. Because *international marketing* implies dealing with a number of different cultures, the importance of this factor is obvious. International marketers must study the culture of the societies in which they operate and adapt to its beliefs, values, attitudes, habits, and forms of behavior.

INDEX